EVERYDAY HEBREW

EVERYDAY HEBREW

Twenty-nine simple
conversations with English translation and
full grammatical introduction

By

CHAIM RABIN
Ph.D. (Lond.), Dipl.O.S.

PHILADELPHIA
DAVID McKAY COMPANY
WASHINGTON SQUARE

Printed in U. S. A.

TO

MY MOTHER

who inspired me with her love for the Hebrew language
and gave me unfailing encouragement in
composing this book

CONTENTS

Foreword	page 9
Grammatical Introduction	13
Short Phrases	62
Conversations	64
1. In Tel Aviv harbour	64
2. At the Customs House	66
3. At the "Egged" Office	68
4. At the restaurant	70
5. Meeting a friend	72
6. Conversation in the coach	74
7. In Jerusalem	76
8. At the parents' house	78
9. On the 'phone	80
10. Dress problems	82
11. In a shop	84
12. The theatre	88
13. Rachel is ill	90
14. Travel plans	92
15. At the Kibbutz	96
16. The sisters meet	98
17. In the chicken-run	100
18. Haifa. At the hotel	102
19. Interview with an employer	104
20. Flat hunting	106
21. Equipping the home	108
22. The furniture arrives	110
23. At the "Tnuva"	112
24. In the new home	114
25. Visitors	118
26. Political conversation	120
27. Engaging a maid	122
28. Simon joins the A.R.P. organization	124
29. Epilogue	126

FOREWORD

HEBREW is the oldest of all living languages. Its earliest written documents date from the ninth century B.C. It has changed so little since then that the text of those inscriptions is intelligible to a Palestinian schoolboy, and if a Jew of that time were to arise to-day he would be able to understand a newspaper, apart from the many new ideas and modes of thought necessarily strange to him.

Spoken Hebrew, however, is the youngest of all languages. Until the nineties of the last century, Hebrew was only used in writing, and its revival as everyday speech is mainly due to the efforts of one man, Eliezer Ben Yehuda (d. 1922). Now it is the living tongue of more than half a million Jews in Palestine and outside it.

As in every language, the spoken form of Hebrew differs in many respects from the written style. It is not only simpler, but in some ways richer and more expressive. With its brevity and familiarity it appeals more directly to the mind than the sonorous and balanced sentences of the literary language. But the student of Hebrew will search for this language in vain in his books because so far it has been denied admission to the realm of literature. Even the dialogue in novels is in strict literary Hebrew. Yet an acquaintance with the style of ordinary conversation is not only useful for those who are about to go to Palestine, it is also most helpful for the student whose main interest lies in reading. Being simpler, colloquial texts will provide him with easy reading matter through which he can become familiar with all important features and words of the language. Then he can attempt more confidently to overcome the additional difficulties of literary texts.

The conversations in this book aim at providing reading-material of that sort. They do not constitute a phrase book and do not profess to help one in every situation in life, nor do they present a short cut to speaking without the trouble of learning the language. All they are intended to do is to acquaint the reader with the most commonly used phrases and constructions which form the groundwork of both the spoken and the written language. They are not designed for the complete beginner, but for those who already know some Hebrew, biblical or modern, and wish to enlarge or refresh their knowledge.

There are many varieties of spoken language, ranging from slang to bookish talk. It is clear that for the foreigner it is best to learn the conversational language of the educated, which avoids both these extremes. In Hebrew, however, there is a special consideration, for the spoken language is still in course of development, many of its features are not yet officially recognized and where it differs from established grammatical standards it is considered faulty although even educated speakers use such ungrammatical forms. For the purposes of this book, it appeared therefore better to conform to established grammar throughout, since this is what would be expected from the educated newcomer. Only residence in the country will teach him when he may take liberties with grammar. The current conversational deviations from grammar have, however, been noted in the introduction.

The choice of words, on the other hand, is as far as possible strictly colloquial. Foreign words have been freely admitted as they are currently employed in conversation and are often difficult for the stranger because of their hebraized form or their changed meaning.

The grammatical introduction has been added to make up for the complete lack of any systematic grammar in English of modern, as distinct from biblical, Hebrew. The differences between the two are mainly in the field of syntax, and for this reason the introduction concentrates on syntactical matters, as well as on other things which are not found in the usual school grammars. On the other hand the inflexion of noun and verb has been dealt with very briefly, aiming more at explaining the principles than the details, and on many points the reader will find no information at all. The reasons for this deviation from general practice are, firstly, that adequate treatments of these subjects can be found in any good grammar of classical Hebrew, secondly, that for the intermediate student, for whom this book is destined, it is more important to master syntax and style. For morphological details he can still rely on the dictionary. The systematic study of morphology, based on the theory of pointing, is best left for the third or fourth year. For the same reason, the vowel signs have at this stage been treated merely as a help for reading without going into the differences between signs that are pronounced the same. The Dagesh has been placed only in ב, כ and פ.

The introduction contains some of the author's own observations. No credit is claimed for these, but if he has erred he will be grateful for correction.

To make the best use of this book, the student should begin by reading each conversation carefully with the help of the translation, referring to the grammar whenever he is in doubt and not only where references are given in the footnotes. When he can account to himself for the meaning and form of each Hebrew word, he should confront each phrase as a whole with the corresponding English one and observe how the two languages differ in expressing the same notion. Needless to say, he must make sure that he is certain of the correct pronunciation of each word in the unpointed text. The grammatical introduction should be read through as a whole when the student is about half through the book.

Above all, try to use your knowledge in actual speech. It is only if you use the words and phrases yourself, in your own life, that they will have real meaning for you. Speaking Hebrew is not at all difficult, as this book will show you. However little you can speak you will find much greater pleasure in reading when the words mean something actual to you.

I wish to thank here Dr. Stein, Lecturer in Hebrew at University College, London, Mr. S. W. D. Rowson, LL.B., Mr, Z. Vardy, LL.B., who have given me valuable advice and criticism, Mr. S. Keyes, who revised the English of the conversations, and Miss C. Rogers, M.A., who corrected the English style of the introduction, as well as all other friends who have given me advice and encouragement in writing this book.

GRAMMATICAL INTRODUCTION

§ 1. The Alphabet

Letter	Final form	Sound	Name	Numerical value	Letter	Final form	Sound	Name	Numerical value
א		*None*	אָלֶף	1	ל		l	לָמֶד	30
ב		b, v	בֵּית	2	מ	ם	m	מֵם	40
ג		g	גִימֶל	3	נ	ן	n	נוּן	50
ד		d	דָלֶת	4	ס		s	סָמֶךְ	60
ה		h	הֵא	5	ע		*None*	עַיִן	70
ו		v, u, o	וָו	6	פ	ף	p, f	פֵּא	80
ז		z	זַיִן	7	צ	ץ	ts	צָדִי	90
ח		ch	חֵית	8	ק		k	קוֹף	100
ט		t	טֵית	9	ר		r	רֵישׁ	200
י		y, i, e	יוֹד	10	ש		sh, s	שִׁין	300
כ	ך	k, ch	כַּף	20	ת		t	תָו	400

Pronunciation

§ 2. א and ע have no sound of their own. They indicate the presence of a vowel at the beginning or end of a word, or following upon another vowel as in שָׁעוֹן **sha–on** *watch*, בֵּאוּר **be–ur** *explanation*. When they come immediately after a consonant, without an intervening vowel, the vowel following them begins a new syllable, and must be sounded as clearly distinct from the preceding consonant, e.g. חֶמְאָה **chem–a** *butter*, מִסְעָדָה **mis–ada** *restaurant*.

ט and ת are not pronounced like the English t, but with the tip of the tongue touching the back of the teeth.

צ is like **ts** in **cats**.

ח and כ have a scraping sound, produced by raising the back of the tongue against the roof of the mouth. It is the same as the Yiddish, German or Scottish **ch**.

The two values of שׁ are in pointed script distinguished by means of a dot: שׁ is **sh** and שׂ is **s**.

§ 3. The two values of ב, כ, פ are in pointing distinguished by a dot in the letter, called Dagesh.[1] Without the Dagesh, they are **v, ch, f** (soft sound), with it **b, k, p** (hard sound). The following rules will help one to pronounce them correctly when reading unpointed script:

(*a*) They are always hard at the beginning of a word, except when preceded by -בְּ *in*, -כְּ *like*, -לְ *to*, וּ or וְ *and*.

(*b*) They are always soft at the end of a word.

(*c*) They are always soft when they occur immediately after a consonant beginning a word, as in צִפְתָּ, תְּבוּנָה.

(*d*) In nouns they are usually hard when they follow a consonant, as in מִדְבָּר, except in the case mentioned under (*c*) and when they belong to a suffix, as in בֵּיתְכֶם. They are mostly soft when they precede a consonant. Between vowels they may be either hard or soft, and no rule can be given.

(*e*) In verbs, the third root-letter is always soft (except in ע״ע and quadriliterals, see § 97). When ב, כ, פ occur as second root-letter they are hard in all forms except the past tense of the Kal and the future tense of the Nif'al (see § 88).

The Vowels

§ 4. The Hebrew script writes the consonants only, and suggests some vowels (see § 5). If it is desired to indicate the vowels it is done by signs above and below the preceding consonants. This is called **Nikkud** or **pointing**.

Hebrew vowels are rather different from those of English. The best thing is to learn them from a Hebrew speaker, but for those who have no opportunity to do so the nearest English vowels are indicated below. The German or French vowels

---

[1] In this book the Dagesh has been placed only in these three letters, as in other letters it has to-day no influence on pronunciation. Actually it can stand in most letters, and is of two kinds: the strong Dagesh, which originally indicated doubling of a letter, and the light Dagesh, which showed the hard sound of the above three letters, and ג, ד, ת.

are more similar to the Hebrew ones, though not quite the
same. In the following list, the vowel signs are put to the
letter א in order to show their position:

Signs	Similar to	Transcription
אִי אִ	ee in meet	i
אֵי אֵ	a in gate	é
אֶ אֶי אֵ	e in get	e
אַ אָ אֲ	a in father	a
א אָ אוֹ אֳ	aw in law	o
אֻ אוּ	u in put (but with rounded lips)	u
אְ	Sign for absence of vowel	

NOTE 1. ָ is pronounced o in a few words only, of which
the most frequent are: כֹּל kol *all*, אָמְנָם omnam *indeed*,
צָהֳרַיִם tsohorayim *mid-day*, חָכְמָה chochma *wisdom*, תָּכְנִית
tochnit *plan*, קָרְבָּן korban *sacrifice*, but not, as some do, in
צָרְפַת tsarfat *France*.

NOTE 2. When ח, ה[1] or ע comes at the end of the word
after any vowel other than a, an a is inserted before it.
Contrary to the general rule, this a is placed under the consonant it precedes: רוּחַ ruach, גָּבֹהַּ gavoah.

NOTE 3. For purposes of grammatical analysis ֳ, ֲ, ֱ
are equivalent to ְ. They appear only with א, ה, ח, ע, ר.

§ 5. The vowels are indicated only in the Bible, prayer
books, children's books and poetry. All normal Hebrew print
is unpointed. It is therefore most important to learn words
so that one can recognize, and correctly pronounce, them
without the vowel signs. This is made easier by the fact that
a large number of the vowels are determined by grammar, so
that a sound knowledge of its rules is a valuable help in reading.
Moreover, the י and ו which form part of some of the above
symbols are kept in unpointed writing and suggest the presence
of i or é, resp. o or u, while ה or א at the end of a word

---

[1] The dot (Mappik) shows that a ה at the end of the word is a true
consonant and not merely an orthographic device to write a final vowel.

mostly point to an **a** or **e**. In order further to facilitate
reading, it is usual in unpointed script to add ו or י where
these do not appear in pointing (i.e. ו for **u, o,** י for **i, é**), as in
בוקר for בֹּקֶר, קיבל for קִבֵּל. Consonantal ו (**v**) and י (**y**) are
often distinguished by writing וו and יי, e.g. ציר is צִיר *delegate*,
butצייר is צַיָּר *painter*.

§ 6. Accent

The accent falls in most words on the last syllable. In a
few it is on the syllable before the last. Such words are in
the following indicated by ˋ. The most important among
them are words with ֶ in the last syllable, the forms of the
past tense ending in **-ti, -ta** and **-nu,** some suffix pronouns,
and the dual-ending **-ayim.**

§ 7. Division of Words

Words consisting of a single letter are written together
with the following word: -בְּ *in,* -דְ *of,*[1] -הַ *the,* -הֲ question
particle, -וְ, -וּ *and,* -כְּ *like,* -לְ *to,* -מִ, -מֵ *from,* -שֶׁ *that.* For compound nouns, see § 25.

§ 8. Abbreviations

Abbreviations of one word are marked by an apostrophe
after the last letter: 'גב for גְּבֶרֶת *Mrs.* 'ה for הָאָדוֹן *Mr.*
Combinations of two or more words have a double apostrophe
before the last letter: א"י for אֶרֶץ־יִשְׂרָאֵל *Palestine,* אעפ"כ for
אַף עַל פִּי כֵן *nevertheless.* Initials of names are marked by full
stops as in English, so is ה.נ.א. *A.R.P.* and דר. *Dr.*

§ 9. Use of the Letters as Number-signs

For dates, pagination, etc., the letters are often employed,
with the numerical values indicated in § 1. Numbers not in
the list are made up by combinations, as נ"ג 53, שע"א 371,
תקצ"ו 596. **15** and **16** are expressed by ט"ו and ט"ז as
the regular writings would form parts of the Divine Name.

The Jewish years are always written with letters, the

[1] Aramaic, occurs only in some idioms.

thousands being omitted: תַּרְצָ"ט 5699, תָּשַׁ"ב 5702. If we want to find the year A.D. corresponding to any Jewish year, we add 1239 for the first 3 months and 1240 for the rest of the year. Thus (5)699 is 1938-9.

§ 10. The Spelling of Foreign Words

European t is written ט, **th** as ת, **k** as ק, **ch** in Greek or German words as כ. The English ending **-tion** appears as -צְיָה, as in רִיאַקְצְיָה *reaction*; **-y** is mostly -יָה, as in הִיסְטוֹרְיָה *history*.

Sounds not found in Hebrew are indicated by the nearest Hebrew letter with an apostrophe: צֶ׳רְצִ׳יל *Churchill*, ג׳וֹרג׳ *George*, סַבּוֹטַאז׳ *sabotage*. **o** and **u** are shown by ו, **i** and **e** by י, **a** often by א. In foreign names, אֶ is sometimes used for **e**, as גֶּארִינג *Goering*.

§ 11. Punctuation

The signs are the same as in English, but inverted commas are placed one below and one above: " ,,. There is no fixed usage as yet, but it is advisable to use the comma as sparingly as possible. No comma is put after an adverbial phrase opening a sentence as is often done in English.

THE PRONOUN

Personal Pronouns

§ 12. Hebrew has two sets of pronouns. The one, the independent pronouns, is used as subject of the sentence, the other, the suffix pronouns, is used when the pronoun is dependent on something, whether it be a noun (possessive), a verb (as object), or a preposition. One says: אַתָּה הוֹלֵךְ *you go*, but בֵּיתְ-ךָ *your house*, רְאִיתִי-ךָ *I saw you*, עִמָּ-ךְ *with you*. The suffix pronouns appear in two different forms, one with nouns in the singular, verbs and most prepositions, the other with nouns in the plural and some prepositions (see § 63).

17

§ 13.

	Independent Pronouns	Suffix Pronouns With singular	With plural	
I	אֲנִי (אָנֹכִי)	־ִי[1]	־ַי	me, my
you (m.)	אַתָּה	־ְךָ	־ֶיךָ	you, your
you (f.)	אַתְּ	־ֵךְ	־ַיִךְ	you, your (f.)
he	הוּא	־וֹ	־ָיו	him, his
she	הִיא	־ָהּ	־ֶיהָ	her
we	אֲנַחְנוּ (אָנוּ)	־ֵנוּ	־ֵינוּ	us, our
you (pl.)	אַתֶּם	־ְכֶם	־ֵיכֶם	you, your
you (pl. f.)	אַתֶּן	־ְכֶן	־ֵיכֶן	you, your (f.)
they	הֵם	־ָם	־ֵיהֶם	them, their
they (f.)	הֵן	־ָן	־ֵיהֶן	them, their (f.)

Thus from עֵט *a pen*, we form עֵטִי *my pen*, עֵטָהּ *her pen*, עֵטַי *my pens*, עֲטֵיהֶם *their pens*. Many nouns undergo changes in their vocalization when these pronouns are attached to them; see §§ 39–48.

The suffix pronouns combine with the endings of verbal forms, and often change their own form as well as that of the endings. It would be beyond the scope of this introduction to explain these. In conversation and ordinary writing one nearly always employs the alternative forms אוֹתִי, אוֹתְךָ, etc. (see § 114).

Forms of Address

§ 14. The usual form of addressing a person is in the second person singular, but when speaking to a stranger or a person one wishes to treat with respect, one often uses the third person singular, and employs אֲדוֹנִי *Sir* or גְּבִרְתִּי *Madam* instead of the personal pronoun, e.g. הַאִם אֲדוֹנִי יִהְיֶה בְּבֵיתוֹ מָחָר? *will you be at home tomorrow, sir?*, lit. *will my master be at his house?*

[1] With verbs ־נִי.

Demonstrative Pronouns

§ 15. *This:* זֶה, fem. זֹאת, pl. (both genders) אֵלֶה follows the noun. Either both זֶה and the noun have the article or both are without it: אִישׁ זֶה or הָאִישׁ הַזֶּה *this man*, without any difference in meaning.

That: הַהוּא fem. הַהִיא pl. masc. הַהֵם pl. fem. הַהֵן follows the noun, which must always have the article: הָאִישׁ הַהוּא *that man*.

With expressions of time, the article is used for *in this, this:* הַשָּׁנָה *this year*, הַיּוֹם *to-day*, הָעֶרֶב *to-night*.

The same: אוֹתוֹ, fem. אוֹתָהּ, pl. אוֹתָם, fem. אוֹתָן precedes the noun, which must have the article: אוֹתוֹ הָאִישׁ *the same man*.

In literary style, אוֹתוֹ, etc., but without the article, means *that:* אוֹתוֹ אִישׁ *that man*. The literary language possesses a further pronoun: הַלָּז, fem. הַלָּזוּ, pl. הַלָּלוּ, which means *that there*, and is constructed like הַהוּא.

§ 16. *Another* (= a different one) is אַחֵר, fem. אַחֶרֶת, pl. אֲחֵרִים, אֲחֵרוֹת, following the noun: בַּיִת אַחֵר *another house*, הָאֲנָשִׁים הָאֲחֵרִים *the other people*. *Another* (= an additional one) is עוֹד preceding the noun: קַח עוֹד כּוֹס תֵּה *have another cup of tea*. When *different* means nothing but *another* it is אַחֵר e.g. זֶה עִנְיָן אַחֵר *that is a different matter*, but where a comparison is implied, the adjective שׁוֹנֶה is used: תֵּל־אָבִיב שׁוֹנָה מִירוּשָׁלַיִם *Tel Aviv is different from Jerusalem*, also עִנְיָנִים שׁוֹנִים *various matters*. *Other than* is זוּלַת־.

Interrogative Pronouns and Adverbs

§ 17. מִי *who?* מַה *what?* אֵיזֶה, fem. אֵיזוֹ *which?* אֵיזֶה בַּיִת *which house?* מָתַי *when?* כַּמָּה *how much?, how many?* אֵיךְ (literary also כֵּיצַד, הֵיאַךְ) *how?* לָמָה, מַדּוּעַ *why?* אֵיפֹה, אַיֵּה *where?* מֵאַיִן *from where?* לְאָן (literary also הֵיכָן) *where to?*

These words are not used in relative clauses, as *the man who came* or *the place where I was*. For these see § 126. *How* in exclamations is כַּמָּה, e.g. כַּמָּה נֶחְמָד *how nice!* *What a* is אֵיזֶה, e.g. אֵיזוֹ חֻצְפָּה *what an impertinence!*

19

Indefinite Pronouns and Adverbs

§ 18. מִישֶׁהוּ *somebody*, דְּבַר־מָה, מַשֶּׁהוּ *something*, אֵיזֶה fem. אֵיזוֹ *some*, as in אֵיזֶה חֵלֶק *some part*. בְּאֵיזֶה מָקוֹם *somewhere*, פַּעַם *sometime, once upon a time*, לִפְעָמִים *sometimes*. In some idioms, *some* is expressed by suffixed מַה: זְמַן־מַה *for some time*, בְּמִדַּת־מָה *to some extent*.

כָּל אִישׁ *every man*, כָּל הָאִישׁ *the whole man*, כָּל הָאֲנָשִׁים *all men*, כָּל אֶחָד, כֻּלָּם *everybody*, הַכֹּל *everything*. *Every single* is expressed by repeating the noun: כָּל אִישׁ וָאִישׁ *every single man*. אֲנָשִׁים אֲחָדִים *some people, a few people*, but אֲנָשִׁים מוּעָטִים *few people* (=not many).

Various Pronominal Expressions

§ 19. *Own* is expressed by repeating the independent pronoun after the suffixed one: אַרְצֵנוּ אָנוּ *our own country*, אִמּוֹ הוּא *his own mother*.

Self is עֶצֶם with suffix pronouns: רָאִיתִי זֹאת בְּעַצְמִי *I saw it myself*, חִנֵּךְ אֶת עַצְמוֹ *he educated himself*. As object of verbs, however, it is often rendered by the special reflexive form, the Hitpaʻel (§ 89): הִתְגַּלַּחְתִּי *I shaved myself*, הִתְנַגַּבְתִּי *I dried myself*. *By one's self* (=without company) is לְבַד with suffix pronouns: בָּא לְבַדּוֹ *he came by himself*, but בָּא בְּעַצְמוֹ *he came himself*.

§ 20. *Each other* is זֶה...זֶה, fem. זוֹ...זוֹ, e.g. רָאוּ זֶה אֶת זֶה *they saw each other*, דִּבַּרְנוּ זֶה עִם זֶה *we spoke to each other*. In literary style the same is also expressed by אִישׁ...אָחִיו, literally *a man...his brother*, fem. אִשָּׁה...אֲחוֹתָהּ, and אִישׁ...רֵעֵהוּ, e.g. הֵם עוֹזְרִים אִישׁ לְאָחִיו *they help each other*, לֹא הֵבִינוּ אִישׁ אֶת שְׂפַת רֵעֵהוּ *they did not understand each other's language*. With some verbs, the Hitpaʻel expresses reciprocity, see § 89.

Negative Pronouns and Adverbs

§ 21. The following pronouns, etc. are not negative in themselves, but they need a negative sentence to complete their meaning. Thus אִישׁ *a man* means *nobody* in a phrase like אִישׁ לֹא בָּא *nobody came*, or *anybody* in אַל תְּסַפֵּר זֹאת לְאִישׁ *don't tell it to anyone*. Another negation (see § 112) is always needed.

שׁוּם, אַף mean *no*, *not a*, as in אֵין לִי שׁוּם כֶּסֶף *I have no money*. אַף אֶחָד is used for *nobody*, שׁוּם דָּבָר, כְּלוּם for *nothing*, בְּשׁוּם מָקוֹם *nowhere*, אַף פַּעַם *never*. לְעוֹלָם means *never* when speaking of the future, מֵעוֹלָם (or מִיָמַי with suffix pronouns) when speaking of the past. Thus one might say מִיָמַי לֹא הָיִיתִי שָׁם וּלְעוֹלָם לֹא אֵלֵךְ לְשָׁם *I have never been there, and will never go there*.

THE NOUN

§ 22. Most Hebrew nouns are formed from **roots** in accordance with definite **patterns**. Several nouns can be formed from one and the same root after various patterns. They will all have a certain common element of meaning, which we call the root-meaning. Thus the words: כְּתָב *script*, כְּתִיב *spelling*, מְכוֹנַת־כְּתִיבָה *typewriter*, מִכְתָּב *letter*, כַּתָּב *correspondent*, כְּתֹבֶת *address*, כְּתֻבָּה *marriage document*, all have in common the three letters כ, ת, ב and some connection with the idea of writing. The same are also found in the verbs לִכְתֹּב *to write*, לְהַכְתִּיב *to dictate*, לְהִתְכַּתֵּב *to carry on a correspondence*. We say, therefore, that all these nouns and verbs are **derived** from the root כתב, meaning *to write*. Similarly מָקוֹם *place*, קוֹמָה *stature*, קָמָה *standing corn*, תְּקוּמָה *rising*, קוֹמְמִיוּת *upright*, לָקוּם *to stand up*, לְהָקִים *to erect* are all derived from a root ק(ו)ם with the meaning *to stand, to rise*. Some roots have more than one meaning, such as ספר, which means *to tell, to count*, and *to cut one's hair*.

§ 23. As the examples show, roots consist only of consonants.[1] The vowels of the word, together with any prefixes

---

[1] Roots consist of three, four, or rarely five consonants. When one of the root letters is weak (see § 95), forms may arise which contain only two or even one root-letter.

and suffixes, constitute the pattern of the word. Thus מַפְתֵּחַ
key, מַזְלֵג *fork*, מַסְרֵק *comb* all have a prefix -מַ and the vowel é
after the second root-letter. To describe the pattern, we
substitute the standard root פעל (meaning *to do*) and say
that three nouns are formed according to the pattern
מַפְעֵל.

These patterns (ca. 30 in number) not only help us to
describe a form unambiguously, they also often give us a
clue to its meaning. Thus we find that all the three מַפְעֵל
nouns mentioned denote *tools*. When we now find a new noun
מַכְתֵּב, we may conclude that it must denote *a tool for writing*,
as in fact it does, namely a *slate pencil*.

Other patterns which carry a definite meaning are פַּעֶלֶת
for diseases, as נַזֶּלֶת *running cold*, שַׁעֶלֶת *whooping cough*,
גַּרְעֶנֶת *stye*; also פִּעָלוֹן for abstracts, as כִּשָׁרוֹן *ability*, זִכָּרוֹן
memory, כִּשָׁלוֹן *failure* (but עִפָּרוֹן *pencil* is concrete), פֹּעַל
denoting qualities, as יֹשֶׁר *honesty*, לֹבֶן *whiteness*, אֹרֶךְ *length*.
פַּעָל denotes tradesmen, as סַבָּל *porter*, סַפָּר *barber*, צַיָּר *painter*.
פַּעְלָן also denotes trades, or persons particularly addicted to
something, as חַלְבָּן *milkman*, סַפְרָן *librarian*, לַמְדָן *a learned
man*, פַּחְדָן *a coward*. The other patterns do not have such a
clear element of meaning, and there are some words formed
after the above patterns which do not fit their meanings.
They help, however, in understanding and remembering
words, and in forming new ones.

It is nearly always worth while to try to discover the
root of a new word, as this will show its connections with
other words and make it easier to memorize.

§ 24. Certain suffixes are added to existing words without
changing their form. One is -וּת which forms abstracts, as
עִתּוֹנוּת *press*, from עִתּוֹן *newspaper*, צִיּוֹנוּת *Zionism*, קַלּוּת *ease*,
from קַל *easy*. -יָה forms words for institutions like עִירִיָּה
town-council, from עִיר *town*, נַקְנִיקִיָּה *sausage shop*, from נַקְנִיק
sausage, or for utensils, like חֲנֻכִּיָּה *Chanukah lamp*, מִטְרִיָּה
umbrella, from מָטָר *rain*. -וֹן, fem. -ֶנֶת, and -ִית, form diminu-

22

tives, as יַלְדֹּנֶת little girl, כַּפִּית teaspoon, from כַּף spoon, מַפִּית serviette, from מַפָּה table-cloth.

§ 25. Compound Nouns

Composition of two nouns, as in *lightship*, does not exist. Its place is taken by the genitive with Smichut (see § 36). כַּדּוּרֶגֶל football (for כַּדּוּר רֶגֶל) is only an apparent exception. In the plural, it is treated like any other Smichut: כַּדּוּרֵי רֶגֶל.

Verbs can be compounded with nouns, as in מַדחֹם *thermometer* (lit. *measure-heat*), רָמקוֹל *megaphone* (lit. *raise-voice*).

Peculiar to Hebrew is the method of connecting two nouns by -וְ *and*, and to treat them as a new word, with a meaning quite distinct from that of the two components, e.g. עוֹבְרִים וְשָׁבִים *passers-by* (lit. *passers-and-returners*), מַשָּׂא וּמַתָּן *negotiations* (lit. *carrying-and-giving*), דִּין וְחֶשְׁבּוֹן *report* (lit. *judgment-and-account*).

§ 26. Gender

There are two genders, masculine and feminine. Feminine are all nouns ending in וּת-, ית-, ת-, ת-, ה-, ה-, except לַיְלָה *night*, שֶׁלְיָה *apprentice*, and שֵׁרוּת *service*.[1] Other nouns are masculine. The following nouns, however, are feminine without having feminine endings:

(a) Words denoting females, as אֵם *mother*, אָחוֹת *sister*, רָחֵל *ewe*.

(b) Names of towns and countries.

(c) Parts of the body that exist in pairs, as רֶגֶל *foot*, זְרוֹעַ *arm*.

(d) The words mentioned in the list.

אֶבֶן stone	אֵשׁ fire	דְּיוֹ ink (also m.)[3]
אוֹת letter of ABC[2]	בְּאֵר well	דֶּרֶךְ way (also m.)
אֶרֶץ country	גָּדֵר fence	דָּת religion

[1] Similarly all verbal nouns Pi'el of roots of which the last letter is ת.
[2] But אוֹת *sign*, pl. אוֹתוֹת, is masculine.
[3] Words which may be of either gender are to-day nearly always treated as feminine.

זָקָן beard (also m.)	נַעַל shoe	צְפַרְדֵּעַ frog
חֶרֶב sword	נֶפֶשׁ soul	קַרְקַע soil (also m.)
בַּד jar (also m.)	סַכִּין knife	קֶרֶן fund, horn
כַּף spoon, palm	עִיר town	רוּחַ wind, spirit (also m.)
לָשׁוֹן tongue, language	עֶצֶם bone	
	עֵת time	שַׁבָּת Sabbath
כֶּתֶר crown	פָּנִים face (also m.)	שָׂדֶה field
מַחַט needle	פַּעַם a time[1]	שֶׁמֶשׁ sun (also m.)
מִכְנָסַיִם trousers	צִפּוֹר bird	

§ 27. The Plural

The plural is formed by attaching ־ים to nouns without feminine endings, and ־וֹת to nouns with feminine endings, whatever the real gender may be. All nouns have the same gender in the plural as in the singular.

The feminine endings ־ָה, ־ֶת, ־ַ are dropped before the ־וֹת is attached: חַיָּה animal, pl. חַיּוֹת, רַכֶּבֶת train, pl. רַכָּבוֹת. The ת- is kept in דֶּלֶת door, רֶפֶת cowshed, לֶפֶת turnip, רֶשֶׁת net, which form דְּלָתוֹת, etc. Nouns ending in ־ִית form the plural in ־ִיּוֹת, those in ־ִית have ־ִיוֹת, e.g. חֲנוּת shop, pl. חֲנוּיוֹת, מַפִּית serviette, pl. מַפִּיוֹת, but ת is kept in שֵׁרוּתִים services and בְּרִיתוֹת alliances. Of חָזִית front, the correct plural is חֲזִיּוֹת, but only חֲזִיתוֹת is used in Palestine now, to avoid confusion with the plural of חֲזִיָּה, vest.

Nouns ending in ־ֶה drop this before taking ־ים or ־וֹת, e.g. עוֹלֶה immigrant, pl. עוֹלִים, שָׂדֶה field, pl. שָׂדוֹת.

Some nouns ending in ־ָה or ־ֶה form the plural in ־ָאוֹת, as סִיסְמָה slogan: סִיסְמָאוֹת; דֻּגְמָה example, model, pl. דֻּגְמָאוֹת; מַשְׁקֶה a drink: מַשְׁקָאוֹת.

§ 28.
Over a hundred nouns without feminine endings take ־וֹת in the plural (without of course affecting their

---

[1] French *fois*, German *mal*.

gender), e.g. אָבוֹת *fathers*, חוֹבוֹת *debts*, אֲרָצוֹת *countries* (f.). Most nouns ending in וֹן- have וֹנוֹת- in the plural, as אֲרוֹנוֹת *cupboards*, חֶסְכּוֹנוֹת *savings*, but עִתּוֹנִים *newspapers*. (מָלוֹן *hotel* is in the plural בָּתֵּי מָלוֹן.) Sometimes both plural forms exist with a difference in meaning, such as עֲצָמוֹת *bones*, עֲצָמִים *objects*, both from עֶצֶם.

§ 29. A number of feminine nouns form their plurals in ים-, after dropping the feminine ending, e.g. דְּבוֹרִים, בֵּיצִים, etc.

בֵּיצָה	*egg*	יוֹנָה	*pigeon*	שִׁבֹּלֶת	*ear of corn* (שִׁבֳּלִים)
דְּבוֹרָה	*bee*	לְבֵנָה	*brick*	שָׁנָה	*year*
דְּבֵלָה	*fig-cake*	מִלָּה	*word*	שְׂעוֹרָה	*barley-plant*
דְּלַעַת	*pumpkin* (דְּלוּעִים)	שׁוֹשַׁנָּה	*rose, lily*	תְּאֵנָה	*fig*
חִטָּה	*wheat-plant*	שִׁטָּה	*acacia*	תּוֹלַעַת	*worm*, etc.

§ 30. Irregular plurals:

אִישׁ	*man:*	אֲנָשִׁים[1]	פֶּה *mouth:*	פִּיּוֹת
אִשָּׁה	*woman:*	נָשִׁים	בַּת *daughter:*	בָּנוֹת
אוֹת	*letter:*	אוֹתִיּוֹת	יוֹם *day:*	יָמִים
אָחוֹת	*sister:*	אֲחָיוֹת	רֹאשׁ *head:*	רָאשִׁים
בַּיִת	*house:*	בָּתִּים	פְּרִי *fruit:*	פֵּרוֹת
עִיר	*town:*	עָרִים		

The Dual

§ 31. The dual denotes two of anything, a pair. It is formed by attaching יִם- to the noun. Feminines ending in ה- form the dual in תַיִם-. It can only be formed from the following two classes of nouns:

(a) Parts of the body and articles of clothing that exist in pairs, as עֵינַיִם *eyes*, גַּרְבַּיִם *socks*. These mostly have only

---

[1] But אִישִׁים *personalities*.

a dual and use it even when more than two are intended, e.g. לַסּוּס יֵשׁ אַרְבַּע רַגְלַיִם *the horse has four legs*. Sometimes both dual and plural exist with different meanings, as רַגְלַיִם *feet*, but רְגָלִים *pilgrimage-festivals* (Pesach, Shavuot, and Sukkot), יָדַיִם *hands*, but יָדוֹת *handles*, עֵינַיִם *eyes*, but עֲיָנוֹת *springs of water*.

(b) Divisions of time, as יוֹמַיִם *two days*, שְׁנָתַיִם *two years*. These have, of course, plurals as well, and it is just as correct, though less idiomatic, to say שְׁנֵי יָמִים, etc.

§ 32. Some nouns exist only in the plural or dual, although they denote single objects, as פָּנִים *face*, חַמִּים *hot water*, נִשּׂוּאִים *marriage*, מַיִם *water*, שָׁמַיִם *sky*, מָעוֹת *money*. They are treated in the sentence like plural nouns, e.g. פָּנִים יָפוֹת *a beautiful face*. No further plural can be formed, so that פָּנִים means both *face* and *faces*.

The Article

§ 33. The definite article *the* is -הַ for all genders and numbers. (ב, כ, פ are pronounced hard after it.) Before nouns beginning with the letters א, ה, ע, ר it is written -הָ, before unstressed הָ, חָ, עָ it becomes -הֶ, e.g. הֶחָלוּץ *the Chalutz*, but in the plural הַחֲלוּצִים.

§ 34. When the prepositions -בְּ *in*, -לְ *to*, -כְּ *like* come to stand before the article, the ה is dropped, and the vowel of the article comes under the preposition: בַּבַּיִת *in the house*, לֶהָרִים *to the mountains*.

§ 35. The indefinite article *a* is mostly not expressed at all. When a word with the indefinite article would come in the beginning of a sentence, however, אֶחָד fem. אַחַת *one is* used: אִישׁ אֶחָד נִכְנַס *a man entered*. The same can also be expressed by אֶחָד (אַחַת) with the plural of the noun: אֶחָד הַתַּלְמִידִים *a pupil* (lit. *one of the pupils*).

The Genitive

§ 36. *The house of the man* can be expressed in three ways:

(*a*) By placing the two nouns together, the thing possessed coming first: בֵּית הָאִישׁ. The first noun must never have the article, and suffers certain changes in its vowels (see §§ 39–48) and its endings: ־ִים or ־ַיִם becomes ־ֵי, ־ֶה becomes ־ֵה, and the feminine ending ־ָה is changed to ־ַת.

This construction is called סְמִיכוּת. In conversational style it is mainly restricted to set phrases, corresponding to English compound nouns, like שִׂמְלַת עֶרֶב *evening gown*, פַּקָּח מִקְלָט *shelter warden*, בֵּית סֵפֶר *school*, but in more literary style it can be used for any genitive. Adjectives, though belonging to the first noun, must follow the second, e.g. עֵינֵי הַבַּחוּרָה הַיָּפוֹת *the beautiful eyes of the girl*. When such expressions are put in the plural, only the first word changes its form, unless the sense requires that the second be put in the plural as well: בָּתֵי סֵפֶר, but פַּקָּחֵי מִקְלָטִים (of several shelters).

§ 37. (*b*) The genitive formation most commonly used in colloquial style is by putting שֶׁל *of* between the two nouns. Neither noun changes its form, either may have the article if required, and adjectives can be placed next to the noun to which they refer, e.g. הָעֵינַיִם הַיָּפוֹת שֶׁל הַבַּחוּרָה הַזֹּאת *the beautiful eyes of this girl*.

The possessive suffix pronouns can also be attached to שֶׁל instead of directly to the noun: הַבַּיִת שֶׁלִּי for בֵּיתִי *my house*. The noun must always have the article, unless *a house of mine* is intended. This construction is often helpful because it avoids changing the vowels of the noun, and is therefore most frequently used with words of foreign origin, where the attachment of suffix pronouns is awkward.

§ 38. (*c*) The third construction is with שֶׁל and the appropriate suffix pronoun affixed to the first noun: בֵּיתוֹ שֶׁל הָאִישׁ, בֵּיתָהּ שֶׁל הָאִשָּׁה, בֵּיתָם שֶׁל הָאֲנָשִׁים.

§ 39. Declension

By declension we mean here the changes which the vowels of a noun undergo in its various forms. These are rather complicated. About 90 per cent of Hebrew nouns are declined according to eight main classes, which are enumerated below. As it is, however, not always to be seen from the form of a noun to which class it belongs, and some of the most frequently used words are quite irregular, it is always best to consult a good dictionary when one meets with a new noun.

§ 40. The forms to be considered in declension are:

Singular	Plural
The absolute form	The absolute form
The Smichut form	The Smichut form
The form before the light suffixes –i, –éch, –o, –ah, –énu, –am, –an	The form before the light suffixes –ay, –echa, –ayich, –av, –eha, –énu
The form before the heavy suffixes –cha, –chem, –chen	The form before the heavy suffixes –échem, –échen, –éhem, –éhen

§ 41. Class 1. Masculine and feminine nouns which do not change their vowels. Examples: שִׁיר *song*, עֵט *pen*, זְאֵב *wolf*, אִכָּר *farmer*, מַזְכִּיר *secretary*, כַּדּוּר *ball*, קוֹנְגְרֶס *congress*. The feminine ending הָ- becomes תַ- in the Smichut singular and תָ- before all singular suffixes. Examples: תִּקְוָה *hope*, גְּבִינָה *cheese*, חוֹמָה *wall*, מַנְגִּינָה *melody*. To this class belong all words in -וּת and -ִית.[1]

§ 42. Class 2. Masculine and feminine nouns that have a ֶ in the last syllable (Segolates).[2] The ֶ is lost in the singular before all suffixes and in the plural in Smichut and before heavy suffixes. In all these forms the vowel preceding the ֶ is changed into:

---

[1] Nouns of the pattern פְּעָלוֹן lose the a (and the Dagesh) in all derived forms: כְּשָׁרוֹן *ability*, כִּשְׁרוֹנִי, etc.

[2] When the second or third root-letter is ע, ח or ה, this ֶ becomes ַ.

(a) ֶ, as in כֶּלֶב dog: כַּלְבִּי; מַחְבֶּרֶת exercise-book: מַחְבַּרְתִּי.

(b) ֵ, as in סֵפֶר book: סִפְרִי; גְּבֶרֶת lady: גְּבִרְתִּי; מֶשֶׁק farm: מִשְׁקִי.

(c) ֵ, as in חֵלֶק part: חֶלְקִי; נֶכֶד grandson: נֶכְדִּי; חֲבֶרָה: חֲבֶרְתִּי.

(d) ֹ (pronounced o!) as in בֹּרֶג screw: בָּרְגִי; כְּתֹבֶת address: כְּתָבְתִּי. In the plural, absolute form and before light suffixes, the ָ becomes ֳ: כְּתָבֶיךָ... but כְּתָבְכֶם. סְפָרִים, כְּלָבַי, כְּלָבֶיךָ, etc.,

All nouns with ֶ are in this class except those in § 46 (b). All those with an o preceding the e follow section (d). Those with other vowels preceding the e may follow (a), (b), or (c). The following list shows the section for some of the more frequently used nouns of this class:

(a) מֶלֶךְ king, נֶפֶשׁ soul, דֶּלֶת door, אֶבֶן stone, חֶדֶר room,[1] רֶגֶל foot.

(b) בֶּגֶד coat, דֶּגֶל flag, שֶׁכֶם shoulder, יְבָמָה sister-in-law, פֶּצַע wound, פֶּרַח flower, מֶלַח salt, קֶמַח flour, צֶמַח plant, צֶבַע colour, שֵׂכֶל sense, עֵמֶק valley, סֵמֶל symbol, מֵצַח forehead, עֵסֶק business.

(c) חֵפֶץ desire, עֵגֶל calf, עֵדֶר flock, עֵרֶךְ value.

§ 43. Class 3. Masculine nouns with ָ in the first and ָ or ָ in the second syllable, as דָּבָר word, thing, נָהָר river, חָצֵר courtyard. The first ָ is dropped in all except the absolute singular form: Smichut דְּבַר, חֲצַר, suffixes: דְּבָרִי, חֲצֵרִי, דְּבַרְכֶם, חֲצַרְכֶם, etc., plural דְּבָרִים, חֲצֵרוֹת, דְּבָרַי, חֲצֵרוֹתַי. In the plural Smichut and with heavy suffixes the second vowel is dropped and the first becomes ִ or ַ (if the 1st or 2nd root-letter is ה, ע, ח): דִּבְרֵי, דִּבְרֵיכֶם; נַהֲרוֹת, חַצְרוֹת, חַצְרוֹתֵיכֶם.

§ 44. Class 4. Masculine nouns with ָ or ֵ in the last and any vowel but ָ in the first syllable. The first vowel is preserved throughout.

(a) If the last syllable has ָ, this becomes ַ in the singular in Smichut and before heavy suffixes, and is dropped in the plural in Smichut and before heavy suffixes. Examples: מוֹשָׁב co-operative village: Smichut מוֹשַׁב, suffixes מוֹשָׁבִי, מוֹשַׁבְכֶם, etc.,

---
[1] Smichut חֲדַר

plural מוֹשָׁבִים, Smichut מוֹשְׁבֵי, suffixes מוֹשָׁבַי מוֹשָׁבְךָ, but מוֹשְׁבֵיכֶם, etc. Also סָמָן sign, שֻׁתָּף partner, צַוָּאר neck.

(b) If the last syllable has ֵ, this becomes ְ in the singular before heavy suffixes, and is dropped in all other forms: מַקֵּל stick: מַקְלִי, מַקֶּלְכֶם, מַקְלוֹת, etc. Similarly, שׁוֹמֵר watchman, מַסְמֵר nail, מַעְדֵּר hoe.

§ 45. Class 5. Masculine nouns with ָ in the first and any other vowel in the second syllable, as פָּקִיד official, מָשׁוֹט oar, חָלוּץ Chalutz. The ָ drops out in all forms: פְּקִיד־, פְּקִידִי, פְּקִידִים ,חֲלוּצֵי ,חֲלוּצִים, פְּקִידֵיכֶם, פְּקִידַי־, etc.

§ 46. Class 6. Masculine nouns that originally doubled their final consonant (in our pronunciation this is noticeable only in the hard sound of ב, כ, פ before suffixes). They remain the same in singular Smichut; in all other forms the vowel of the syllable before the suffix becomes:

(a) ַ in אַף nose: אַפִּי, אַפְּךָ, אַפּוֹ. Also קַו line, מָמְתָּק sweet, מַרְבָד carpet, עַפְעָף eyelid, גָּמָל camel, עָצָב nerve, גַּב back, כַּף spoon, etc.

(b) ִ in עֵז goat: עִזִּי, עִזִּים, עִזֵּי, etc. Also אֵם mother, שֵׁן tooth, לֵב heart, צַד side, בַּת daughter, מַס tax, מָגֵן shield, גַּרְזֶן axe, אֱמֶת truth,[1] etc.

(c) ֻ in חֹק law: חֻקִּי, חֻקִּים, etc. Also רֹב majority, חֹם fever, לְאֹם nation, קַרְסֹל ankle.

If the vowel of the first syllable is ְ, it is dropped in all forms: עֲצַבִּים, נְמַלִּים, etc.

§ 47. Class 7. Feminine nouns with two consonants preceding the feminine ending, like יַלְדָּה girl, חֶלְקָה plot, חֹרְשָׁה forest. These are treated like the feminine nouns in class 1, except for the absolute form of the plural, which is יְלָדוֹת, חֲרָשׁוֹת, חֲלָקוֹת.

§ 48. Class 8. Some feminine nouns with ָ or ֵ in the syllable preceding the ending, as מָנָה portion, דְּמָמָה silence,

[1] Contrary to the rule in § 6, the last two words are stressed on the last syllable.

(a) ־ֶ, as in כֶּלֶב *dog*: כַּלְבִּי; מַחְבֶּרֶת *exercise-book*: מַחְבַּרְתִּי.

(b) ־ֵ, as in סֵפֶר *book*: סִפְרִי; גְּבֶרֶת *lady*: גְּבִרְתִּי; מֶשֶׁק *farm*: מִשְׁקִי.

(c) ־ָ, as in חֵלֶק *part*: חֶלְקִי; נֶכֶד *grandson*: נֶכְדִּי; חֲבֵרָה: חֲבֶרְתִּי.

(d) ־ֶ (pronounced o!) as in בֹּרֶג *screw*: בָּרְגִּי; כְּתֹבֶת *address*: כְּתָבְתִּי. In the plural, absolute form and before light suffixes, the ־ֶ becomes ־ָ: סְפָרִים, כְּלָבִים, etc., כְּלָבַי, כְּלָבֶיךָ...but כַּלְבֵּיכֶם.

All nouns with ־ֶ are in this class except those in § 46 (b). All those with an o preceding the e follow section (d). Those with other vowels preceding the e may follow (a), (b), or (c). The following list shows the section for some of the more frequently used nouns of this class:

(a) מֶלֶךְ *king*, נֶפֶשׁ *soul*, דֶּלֶת *door*, אֶבֶן *stone*, חֶדֶר *room*,[1] רֶגֶל *foot*.

(b) בֶּגֶד *coat*, דֶּגֶל *flag*, שֶׁכֶם *shoulder*, יְבֶמֶת *sister-in-law*, פֶּצַע *wound*, פֶּרַח *flower*, מֶלַח *salt*, קֶמַח *flour*, צֶמַח *plant*, צֶבַע *colour*, שֵׂכֶל *sense*, עֵמֶק *valley*, סֵמֶל *symbol*, מֵצַח *forehead*, עֵסֶק *business*.

(c) חֵפֶץ *desire*, עֵגֶל *calf*, עֵדֶר *flock*, עֵרֶךְ *value*.

§ 43. Class 3. Masculine nouns with ־ָ in the first and ־ָ or ־ָ in the second syllable, as דָּבָר *word, thing*, נָהָר *river*, חָצֵר *courtyard*. The first ־ָ is dropped in all except the absolute singular form: Smichut דְּבַר, חֲצַר, suffixes: דְּבָרִי, חֲצֵרִי, דְּבַרְכֶם, חֲצַרְכֶם, etc., plural דְּבָרִים, חֲצֵרוֹת, דְּבָרַי, חֲצֵרוֹתַי. In the plural Smichut and with heavy suffixes the second vowel is dropped and the first becomes ־ִ or ־ֶ (if the 1st or 2nd root-letter is ה, ע, ח): חַצְרוֹתֵיכֶם, חַצְרוֹת, נַהֲרוֹת; דִּבְרֵיכֶם, דִּבְרֵי.

§ 44. Class 4. Masculine nouns with ־ָ or ־ֵ in the last and any vowel but ־ָ in the first syllable. The first vowel is preserved throughout.

(a) If the last syllable has ־ָ, this becomes ־ַ in the singular in Smichut and before heavy suffixes, and is dropped in the plural in Smichut and before heavy suffixes. Examples: מוֹשָׁב *co-operative village*: Smichut מוֹשַׁב, suffixes מוֹשָׁבִי, מוֹשַׁבְכֶם, etc.,

---

[1] Smichut חֲדַר

plural מוֹשָׁבִים, Smichut מוֹשְׁבֵי, suffixes מוֹשָׁבַי מוֹשָׁבֶיךָ, but מוֹשְׁבֵיכֶם, etc. Also סִמָן סִימָן sign, שׁוּתָף partner, צַוָּאר neck.

(b) If the last syllable has ֵ, this becomes ְ in the singular before heavy suffixes, and is dropped in all other forms: מַקֵּל stick: מַקְלִי, מַקֶּלְכֶם, מַקְלוֹת, etc. Similarly, שׁוֹמֵר watchman, מַסְמֵר nail, מַעְדֵּר hoe.

§ 45. Class 5. Masculine nouns with ָ in the first and any other vowel in the second syllable, as פָּקִיד official, מָשׁוֹט oar, חָלוּץ Chalutz. The ָ drops out in all forms: פְּקִיד־, פְּקִידִי, חֲלוּצֵי, פְּקִידֵיכֶם, פְּקִידֵי־, פְּקִידִים, etc.

§ 46. Class 6. Masculine nouns that originally doubled their final consonant (in our pronunciation this is noticeable only in the hard sound of ב, כ, פ before suffixes). They remain the same in singular Smichut; in all other forms the vowel of the syllable before the suffix becomes:

(a) ַ in אַף nose: אַפּוֹ, אַפְּךָ, אַפִּי. Also קַו line, מַמְתָּק sweet, מַרְבָד carpet, עַפְעַף eyelid, גָּמָל camel, עָצָב nerve, גַּב back, כַּף spoon, etc.

(b) ִ in עֵז goat: עִזִּי, עִזִּים, עִזֵּי־, etc. Also אֵם mother, שֵׁן tooth, לֵב heart, צַד side, בַּת daughter, מַס tax, מָגֵן shield, גַּרְזֶן axe, אֱמֶת truth,[1] etc.

(c) ֻ in חֹק law: חֻקִּי, חֻקִּים, etc. Also רֹב majority, חֹם fever, לְאֹם nation, קַרְסֹל ankle.

If the vowel of the first syllable is ְ, it is dropped in all forms: גְּמַלִּים, עֲצַבִּים, etc.

§ 47. Class 7. Feminine nouns with two consonants preceding the feminine ending, like יַלְדָּה girl, חֶלְקָה plot, חֻרְשָׁה forest. These are treated like the feminine nouns in class 1, except for the absolute form of the plural, which is יְלָדוֹת, חֲרָשׁוֹת, חֲלָקוֹת.

§ 48. Class 8. Some feminine nouns with ָ or ֵ in the syllable preceding the ending, as מָנָה portion, דְּמָמָה silence,

[1] Contrary to the rule in § 6, the last two words are stressed on the last syllable.

אֲדָמָה *earth,* לְבֵנָה *brick,* שֵׁנָה *sleep.* These vowels are only kept
in the absolute forms of the singular and plural, and dropped
in all other forms: מְנוֹתִי, מְנָתִי, מְנַת־, מְנוֹת, etc.

Words of the type of דְמָמָה and אֲדָמָה are further transformed into אַרְמַת־, דִּמְמַת־, etc. Many nouns looking just
like these, however, belong to class 1 and do not change
their vowels, as תְּעָלָה *canal,* בַּקָּשָׁה *request,* הַמְצָאָה *invention,*
שְׁאֵלָה *question,* מַסֵּכָה *mask,* etc.

§ 49.
Some frequently used irregular nouns:

אָב *father* and אָח *brother* have ־ִי attached in the singular
Smichut and before suffixes: אָבִיהָ, אָבִיו, אָבִיךָ, אָבִי, אֲבִי־, etc.
אָב has the plural אָבוֹת; the plural of אָח is regular except for
the form אֶחָיו *his brothers.*

בֵּן *son.* Singular Smichut בֶּן, with suff. בְּנִי, בְּנוֹ, etc., but
בִּנְךָ, בִּנְכֶם, plural בָּנִים, Smichut בְּנֵי, with suff. בָּנַי, בָּנֶיךָ, etc.,
but בְּנֵיכֶם, etc.

אִשָּׁה *wife, woman,* Smichut־ אֵשֶׁת, with suff. אִשְׁתִּי, etc. Plural
נָשִׁים, Smichut נְשֵׁי־, with suff. נְשׁוֹתַי, etc.

מָוֶת *death,* Smichut and before suff. מוֹת.

שֵׁם *name,* שְׁמִי, שְׁמוֹ but שִׁמְךָ, שִׁמְכֶם, plural שֵׁמוֹת, Smichut
and before suff. שְׁמוֹת.

The Adjective

§ 50.
Adjectives follow the noun to which they belong
and agree with it in gender and number. If the noun has the
article, the adjective must also have it.

אִישׁ טוֹב *a good man*	אִשָּׁה טוֹבָה *a good woman*
הָאִישׁ הַטּוֹב *the good man*	הָאִשָּׁה הַטּוֹבָה *the good woman*
אֲנָשִׁים טוֹבִים *good men*	נָשִׁים טוֹבוֹת *good women*
הָאֲנָשִׁים הַטּוֹבִים *the good men*	הַנָּשִׁים הַטּוֹבוֹת *the good women*

Proper names and nouns with suffix pronouns attached are
treated as if they had the article: יִצְחָק הַקָּטָן *little Isaac,*

שִׂמְלָתִי הַחֲדָשָׁה *my new frock*. If the noun has the article and the adjective has not, the construction represents a complete sentence, with an *is* implied (§ 99), e.g. הָאִישׁ טוֹב means *the man is good*.

§ 51. The formation of the feminine and plural of adjectives follows the pattern with more regularity than the declension of nouns. Apart from words like טוֹב, where the vowels are not changed, the following classes are often found:

	1	2	3	4	5	6	7
	large	*yellow*	*old*	*dumb*	*dear*	*hard*	*Jewish*
Sing.m.	גָּדוֹל	צָהֹב	זָקֵן	אִלֵּם	יָקָר	קָשֶׁה	יְהוּדִי
Sing.f.	גְּדוֹלָה	צְהֻבָּה	זְקֵנָה	אִלֶּמֶת	יְקָרָה	קָשָׁה	יְהוּדִית
Pl.m.	גְּדוֹלִים	צְהֻבִּים	זְקֵנִים	אִלְּמִים	יְקָרִים	קָשִׁים	יְהוּדִיִּים
Pl.f.	גְּדוֹלוֹת	צְהֻבּוֹת	זְקֵנוֹת	אִלְּמוֹת	יְקָרוֹת	קָשׁוֹת	יְהוּדִיּוֹת

§ 52. Some of the above patterns have a definite meaning. Thus pattern 2 comprises most words for colours, as יָרֹק *green*, וָרֹד *pink* (from וֶרֶד *rose*). In unpointed script these are mostly spelled with a ו and look like words of pattern 1, with which one should therefore beware of confusing them. The only adjectives of pattern 2 not denoting colours are אָרֹךְ *long*, עָגֹל *round*, עָנֹג *tender*, עָרֹם *naked*. Pattern 4 denotes bodily and mental defects, as גִּבֵּן *hunchbacked*, פִּסֵּחַ *limping*, טִפֵּשׁ *silly*. If ב, כ, פ are the second root-letter, they are hard in this pattern, if the second root-letter is ה, ע, ר the first vowel is ֵ, as in קֵרֵחַ *bald*. The pattern פְּעַלְעַל forms diminutives from other adjectives, as קְטַנְטָן *very small*, יְרַקְרַק *greenish*, שְׁמַנְמֹנֶת *buxom*.

The suffix ־ִי, i.e. pattern 7, forms adjectives from practically every noun. The noun is before this suffix in the same form as before light pronoun suffixes (§ 40), e.g. אִישִׁי *personal*, מְקוֹמִי *local*, בֵּיתִי *homely*, שְׁנָתִי *annual*, מַמְלַכְתִּי *govern-*

32

mental, תֵּל אֲבִיבִי *Tel-Avivian.* Of אֶרֶץ יִשְׂרָאֵל both אֶרֶץ־יִשְׂרְאֵלִי and אַרְצִי־יִשְׂרְאֵלִי are in use.

§ 53. Adjectives can without any restriction be used as nouns: זָקֵן *an old man, grandfather,* יָרֹק *a greenhorn,* מְקוֹמִי *a native,* הַגְּדוֹלִים *the great.* When adjectives ending in ־י are used as nouns, their inflexion differs from that of class 7 above: יְהוּדִי *Jew*: pl. יְהוּדִים; יְהוּדִיָּה *Jewess*: pl. יְהוּדִיּוֹת.

Many adjectives are really participles. For their forms see § 97.

Comparison of Adjectives

§ 54. גָּדוֹל *large* נָדוֹל יוֹתֵר or יוֹתֵר נָדוֹל *larger*—נָדוֹל הַיּוֹתֵר or הַגָּדוֹל בְּיוֹתֵר *the largest.* The superlative is in colloquial style also formed by putting הֲכִי before the adjective: הֲכִי נָדוֹל.

In literary style, יוֹתֵר is left out wherever this can be done without causing ambiguity: יוֹסֵף גָּדוֹל מֵאָחִיו *Joseph is bigger than his brother,* תֵּל אָבִיב הַגְּדוֹלָה בְּעָרֵי א״י *Tel Aviv is the largest town in Palestine.*

§ 55. *Than* in comparisons is מִן (see § 62). When the second term of comparison is not expressed, but only implied, מֵאֲשֶׁר must be used: הַחֹם בְּא״י גָּדוֹל מֵאֲשֶׁר בְּאַנְגְלִיָּה *the heat in Palestine is greater than (the heat) in England.*

§ 56. *Like* is -כְּ or כְּמוֹ. *Just like* בְּדִיּוּק כְּמוֹ. *Very large* גָּדוֹל מְאֹד. *not very large* גָּדוֹל בְּיוֹתֵר or לֹא גָּדוֹל בְּיוֹתֵר. *Rather difficult* קָשֶׁה בְּמִקְצָת, *a little difficult* קָשֶׁה לְמַדַּי or דֵּי קָשֶׁה, *too difficult* קָשֶׁה מְדַּי, יוֹתֵר מְדַּי קָשֶׁה.

The Adverb

§ 57. There is no simple means for turning adjectives into adverbs, such as the English suffix *-ly.* Some adverbs are the same as the corresponding adjectives, e.g. יָפֶה *nice, nicely,* קָשֶׁה *heavy, heavily.* Adjectives in ־י mostly form adverbs in ־ית: בְּמִבְיַת *publicly,* זְמַנִּית *temporarily,* עִבְרִית *in Hebrew.* Most adverbs are made up either by vowel changes or by combinations of nouns and prepositions, as the following examples:

טוֹב	good	הֵיטֵיב	well
קַל	easy	בְּנֶקֶל, בְּקַלּוּת	easily
בָּטוּחַ	safe	בֶּטַח	safely
מָהִיר	quick	מַהֵר	quickly
אִטִּי	slow	לְאַט	slowly

These can be learnt only by practice. It is permissible, though not elegant, to avoid this difficulty by using בְּאֹפֶן *in a manner* with the adjective: בְּאֹפֶן קַל *easily*, בְּאֹפֶן בָּרוּר *clearly*.

Some Useful Adverbs

§ 58. There are many adverbs not derived from adjectives. Some of these contribute materially to the idiomatic character of one's style, and are often without any equivalents in other languages. The following small selection may be helpful:[1]

afterwards	אַחֲרֵי־כֵן	backwards	אֲחוֹרָה
again	שׁוּב, מֵחָדָשׁ, עוֹד הַפַּעַם	by the way	דֶּרֶךְ אֲגַב
all the more so	כָּל שֶׁכֵּן	certainly	בְּוַדַּאי
already	כְּבָר	daily	יוֹם יוֹם
altogether	בִּכְלָל	especially	בִּפְרָט
always	תָּמִיד	even	אֲפִילוּ
anyway	מִכָּל מָקוֹם	generally	עַל פִּי רֹב
apart	לְחוּד	gratis	חִנָּם
approximately	בְּעֵרֶךְ, כְּ-	in advance	לְמִפְרֵעַ
at last	סוֹף סוֹף	indeed	אָמְנָם
at least	לְכָל הַפָּחוֹת	intentionally	בְּכַוָּנָה, מִדַּעַת
at once	מִיָּד	just	דַּוְקָא

[1] A few words are included here which are not strictly adverbs.

mainly	בְּעָקָר	simply	סְתָם, פָּשׁוּט
meanwhile	בֵּינְתַיִם	secretly	חֶרֶשׁ, בַּחֲשַׁאי
nearly	כִּמְעַט	so	כֹּה, כָּכָה
nevertheless	אַף עַל פִּי כֵן	so far	עַד הֵנָּה
not yet	טֶרֶם	soon	עוֹד מְעַט, בְּקָרוֹב
now	עַכְשָׁו, עַתָּה	so to say	כַּבְיָכֹל
of course	כַּמּוּבָן	specially	בִּמְיֻחָד
only	רַק, אַךְ	still	עוֹד
on the contrary	אַדְּרַבָּא	suddenly	פִּתְאֹם
onwards	וָאֵילָךְ	then (at that time)	אָז
otherwise	אַחֶרֶת	then (in that case)	אִם כֵּן
outside	בַּחוּץ	therefore	לָכֵן
perhaps	אוּלַי	together	יַחַד
properly	כַּהֹגֶן, כָּרָאוּי	usually	כָּרָגִיל
really	בֶּאֱמֶת	would that	הַלְוַאי

§ 59. The two words הִנֵּה and הֲרֵי serve to draw attention to a statement. They have no equivalent in English. הִנֵּה invites the hearer to convince himself with his own eyes of the fact to be mentioned: הִנֵּה מֹשֶׁה בָּא *there is Moses coming*, הִנְנִי נוֹתֵן לְךָ אֶת זֹאת *I am giving you this*. הֲרֵי on the other hand points out that the hearer is well aware of the fact, and it is really superfluous to mention it: הֲרֵי אָמַרְתָּ כֵּן בְּעַצְמְךָ *didn't you say so yourself?*, הֲרֵי אִי אֶפְשָׁר לְהַמְשִׁיךְ כָּכָה *you'll agree we can't go on like this*. הֲלֹא is used much like הֲרֵי and might be translated in English by *isn't it?* etc., e.g. הֲלֹא רְאִיתִי אוֹתְךָ *I saw you, didn't I?* See also § 117 end.

§ 60. *Only* is expressed by רַק or אַךְ before, or בִּלְבַד, לְבַד after the noun. Often, however, one uses a negative sentence followed by אֶלָּא *except, but*, e.g. אֵין לָהּ אֶלָּא כּוֹבַע אֶחָד *she has only one hat*, לֹא אָמַר זֹאת אֶלָּא בִּצְחוֹק *he only meant it as a joke*.

§ 61. Prepositions

above	לְמַעְלָה מִן	in spite of	לַמְרוֹת, עַל אַף
according to	לְפִי	instead of	בִּמְקוֹם
after	אַחֲרֵי (2)	like	כְּ-, כְּמוֹ
against	נֶגֶד (נֶגְדִּי)	near	עַל יַד
along	לְאֹרֶךְ	of	שֶׁל
among	בֵּין	on	עַל (2)
at (chez)	אֵצֶל (אֶצְלִי)	on behalf of	בְּשֵׁם (בִּשְׁמִי)
because of	מִפְּנֵי (2)	on top of	עַל גַּבֵּי
before	לִפְנֵי (2, לְפָנַי)	opposite	מוּל
behind	מֵאֲחֹרֵי (2)	out of	מִתּוֹךְ
between	בֵּין	outside	מִחוּץ לְ-
by (means of)	בְּ-, בְּדֶרֶךְ	thanks to	הוֹדוֹת לְ
by (passive)	עַל יְדֵי (2)	through	דֶּרֶךְ (דַּרְכִּי)
concerning	עַל אוֹדוֹת (2)	to	לְ- (1), אֶל (2)
during	בְּמֶשֶׁךְ, בִּשְׁעַת	towards	כְּלַפֵּי; לִקְרַאת
except	חוּץ מִן	under	תַּחַת (2)
for	בִּשְׁבִיל, בְּעַד	until	עַד (2)
from	מִן	with (in company of)	עִם (1) אֵת (אִתִּי, 1)
in	בְּ- (1)		
in front of	לִפְנֵי (2)	with (by means of)	בְּ- (1)
inside	בְּתוֹךְ	without	בְּלִי (בִּלְעֲדַי, 2)

§ 62. The form מִן is used before the article only. Before nouns without article, it is -מִ; if the first consonant is א, ה, ח, ע, ר, it is -מֵ; e.g. מֵחֲבֵרִי, מִבֵּיתִי, מִן הַבַּיִת.

§ 63. Pronouns after prepositions are always in the suffix form. With some prepositions (those marked (1) in the above list) the singular suffixes are used with slight differences in form, as in עִם below. The forms that differ from those of ordinary nouns are marked *. Others (marked (2) in the list) take plural suffixes, as עַל. מִן and כְּמוֹ (-כְּ) does not take

36

suffixes) are entirely irregular. The remaining prepositions are originally nouns, and are declined like these. Changes in vowels are indicated in the list.

	(1) *with*	(2) *on*	(3) *from*	(4) *like*
me	עִמִּי	עָלַי	מִמֶּנִּי	כָּמוֹנִי
you	עִמְּךָ	עָלֶיךָ	מִמְּךָ	כָּמוֹךָ
you (f.)	עִמָּךְ *	עָלַיִךְ	מִמֵּךְ	כְּמוֹךְ
him	עִמּוֹ	עָלָיו	מִמֶּנּוּ	כָּמוֹהוּ
her	עִמָּהּ	עָלֶיהָ	מִמֶּנָּה	כָּמוֹהָ
us	עִמָּנוּ *	עָלֵינוּ	מֵאִתָּנוּ	כָּמוֹנוּ
you (pl.)	עִמְּכֶם (לָכֶם)	עֲלֵיכֶם	מִכֶּם	כְּמוֹכֶם
you (f.)	עִמְּכֶן	עֲלֵיכֶן	מִכֶּן	כְּמוֹכֶן
them	עִמָּהֶם *	עֲלֵיהֶם	מֵהֶם	כְּמוֹתָם
them (f.)	עִמָּהֶן *	עֲלֵיהֶן	מֵהֶן	כְּמוֹתָן

§ 64. There are many differences between Hebrew and English in the use of the prepositions, especially after verbs. Many verbs that are in English directly connected with their object require the intervention of a preposition in Hebrew, as לֶאֱחֹז בְּ- *to seize*, לִבְחֹר בְּ- *to choose*, לְהִתְנַבֵּר עַל *to overcome*, לֵהָנוֹת מִן *to enjoy*, לְהַרְגִּישׁ בְּ- *to feel, to notice*, לְהִכָּנֵס אֶל *to enter*, לְהִשְׁתַּמֵּשׁ בְּ- *to use*, לִנְגֹּעַ בְּ- *to touch*, לְהַגִּיעַ אֶל *to reach*, לַעֲזוֹר לְ- *to help*.

Others, again, require a preposition in English, but take a direct object in Hebrew, as לְבַקֵּשׁ *to ask for*, לְחַפֵּשׂ *to look for*. Different prepositions are employed in לְדַבֵּר עִם *to talk to*, לְטַפֵּל בְּ- *to look after*, לְהוֹדוֹת לְמִישֶׁהוּ עַל דְּבַר־מָה *to thank somebody for something*, לְהִתְפַּלֵּל עַל *to pray for*, etc. Note also: הַדָּבָר עוֹלֶה לִי בִּשְׁלֹשָׁה גְרוּשׁ *the thing costs me 3 piastres*.

Special attention must be paid to the different meanings of *with*, e.g. בָּא עִם אָחִיו *he came with his brother*, הִכָּה אוֹתוֹ בְּמַקֵּל *he hit him with a stick*. When *with* means *possessing*, it must be translated by בַּעַל, fem. בַּעֲלַת, e.g. בַּחוּרָה בַּעֲלַת עֵינַיִם שְׁחוֹרוֹת

a girl with dark eyes. In literary style the same can be expressed by Smichut: בַּחוּרָה שְׁחוֹרַת עֵינַיִם.

§ 65. לְ- with the suffix corresponding to the subject of the sentence is used in a number of idiomatic expressions. It does not add anything to the meaning, but merely serves to give the phrase greater weight, e.g. לֶךְ־לְךָ *go away*, דַּע לְךָ *know*, יָשַׁב לוֹ בַּגַּן וְקָרָא *he sat in the garden and read*, חָשַׁבְתִּי לִי *I thought to myself*.

§ 66. Going *to* a place is expressed either by לְ- or אֶל, or by the suffix -ָה (which is always unstressed), e.g. אֲנִי הוֹלֵךְ הַבַּיְתָה *I am going home*, הָעִירָה *to town*, לֵךְ הַחוּצָה *go outside*, אַרְצָה *to earth, to Palestine*, תֵּל־אָבִיבָה *to Tel-Aviv*.

§ 67. Hebrew does not use prepositional phrases as attributes, as in *the book on the table*. A relative clause must be employed: הַסֵּפֶר שֶׁעַל הַשֻּׁלְחָן, lit. *the book which is on the table*. Without the -שֶׁ, the words would mean *the book is on the table*.

Numbers

§ 68. All numbers, except the pure decades *20, 30*, etc., have separate forms for counting masculine and feminine nouns, e.g. שְׁלֹשָׁה אֲנָשִׁים *three men*, but שָׁלֹשׁ נָשִׁים *three women*. For counting without nouns, the feminine numerals are employed.

אֶחָד (אַחַת) *one* follows the noun, all other numbers precede it. With numbers above ten, the noun may be in the singular: עֶשְׂרִים יֶלֶד or עֶשְׂרִים יְלָדִים *twenty children*. The words מִיל *Mil*, גְּרוּשׁ *Piastre*, and אִישׁ when used merely as a counting measure, are always in the singular, e.g. הָיִינוּ חֲמִשָּׁה אִישׁ *we were five persons*, but שְׁלֹשָׁה אֲנָשִׁים וּשְׁתֵּי נָשִׁים *three men and two women*.

Two is שְׁנַיִם (שְׁתַּיִם) when used for pure counting, שְׁנֵי (שְׁתֵּי) when followed by a noun. The other masculine forms of numbers under ten have special Smichut forms when the noun has the article: חֲמִשָּׁה בָתִּים *five houses*, but חֲמֵשֶׁת הַבָּתִּים. These forms are: שְׁמֹנַת, שִׁבְעַת, שֵׁשֶׁת, חֲמֵשֶׁת, אַרְבַּעַת, שְׁלֹשֶׁת, עֲשֶׂרֶת, תִּשְׁעַת. These forms are also employed before *thousand*: שְׁלֹשֶׁת אֲלָפִים *3000*, etc.

§ 69. The ordinals, with the exception of רִאשׁוֹן *first*, are derived from the cardinal numbers after the pattern פְּעִילִי: שְׁלִישִׁי, רְבִיעִי, חֲמִשִׁי, etc. The feminine is in ־ית. For numbers above ten, the ordinals are identical with the cardinal numbers. They are treated like adjectives, i.e. follow the noun and have the article if the noun has it.

§ 70. Fractions: חֵצִי, Smichut חֲצִי, before suffixes חֶצְיִי, etc., *half*, שְׁלִישׁ *third*, רֶבַע *quarter*, חֹמֶשׁ *fifth*. For the other fractions, the feminine ordinals ending in ־ית are used.

§ 71. *Firstly, secondly*, etc. are rendered by the feminine ordinals: רִאשׁוֹנָה and so on. *A trio* שְׁלִישִׁיָה, *a quartet* רְבִיעִיָה. *Triangle* מְשֻׁלָּשׁ, *quadrangle* מְרֻבָּע. *Double* כָּפוּל, *to double* לְהַכְפִּיל.

THE VERB

Tenses

§ 72. Hebrew has three tenses: Past, Present and Future. The past tense indicates the persons by suffixes, the future tense by prefixes (with some suffixes for showing gender and number only).

The present tense distinguishes only gender and number, as it is really a participle, and can be used as such. אֲנִי הוֹלֵךְ means *I am going*; the verb *to be* is implied (see § 98). It must therefore always be accompanied by the personal pronoun. The other two tenses do not need the personal pronouns, since the person is adequately expressed by the forms of the verb itself, and in writing the pronouns should only be used when it is desired to stress them, as in אֲנִי הָלַכְתִּי *it is I who went*. In colloquial style, however, this rule is often violated.

§ 73. The following table shows the suffixes and prefixes of the past and future tenses, and the formation of the present tense. The forms shown are of the verb *to write*.

	Past	*I wrote*	Future	*I shall write*	*I am writing*
I	}-ti	כָּתַבְתִּי	}e-	אֶכְתֹּב	אֲנִי כּוֹתֵב
I (f.)					אֲנִי כּוֹתֶבֶת
you	-ta	כָּתַבְתָּ	ti-	תִּכְתֹּב	אַתָּה כּוֹתֵב
you (f.)	-t	כָּתַבְתְּ	ti- -i	תִּכְתְּבִי	אַתְּ כּוֹתֶבֶת
he	—	כָּתַב	yi-	יִכְתֹּב	הוּא כּוֹתֵב
she	-a	כָּתְבָה	ti-	תִּכְתֹּב	הִיא כּוֹתֶבֶת
we	}-nu	כָּתַבְנוּ	}ni-	נִכְתֹּב	אֲנַחְנוּ כּוֹתְבִים
we (f.)					אֲנַחְנוּ כּוֹתְבוֹת
you	-tem	כְּתַבְתֶּם	ti- -u	תִּכְתְּבוּ	אַתֶּם כּוֹתְבִים
you (f.)	-ten	כְּתַבְתֶּן	ti- -na	תִּכְתֹּבְנָה	אַתֶּן כּוֹתְבוֹת
they	}-u	כָּתְבוּ	yi- -u	יִכְתְּבוּ	הֵם כּוֹתְבִים
they (f.)			ti- -na	תִּכְתֹּבְנָה	הֵן כּוֹתְבוֹת

The suffixes of the past tense are the same in every Hebrew verb. The prefixes of the future tense have the same consonants in all verbs, but the vowels vary: רַגִּישׁ, אֶאֱסֹף, יֵלֵךְ, יִכְתֹּב, יוּכַל, יוֹשִׁיב, יָקוּם. Any differences and irregularities affect only the stem, but not the formation of the persons.

Other Forms

§ 74. There are two infinitives. The absolute infinitive, כָּתוֹב, is to-day only employed in dictionaries and in the construction § 86 (*c*). The other, the construct infinitive, must always be preceded by a preposition, as לִכְתֹּב *to write*.

The construct infinitive can also take suffix pronouns; before these it takes the form -כָּתְב (pron. **kotv-**). The pronouns can, according to the sense, denote either the object, as in לְכָתְבוֹ *to write it*, or the subject, as בְּכָתְבִי *in my writing, while I wrote*. This construction often renders subordinate

40

clauses, without expressing any time. Thus אַחֲרֵי לֶכְתִּי may mean *after I had gone* or *after I will have gone*, similarly לַמְרוֹת לֶכְתּוֹ *although he goes, went* or *will go*.

§ 75. The verbal noun, כְּתִיבָה, means *writing, the manner of writing, the action of writing*, e.g. דִּבּוּרוֹ שׁוֹטֵף *his speech (manner of speaking) is fluent*, קִיֵּם אֶת דִּבּוּרוֹ *he stood by his word (that which he had spoken)*, הַדִּבּוּר הָעִבְרִי חָשׁוּב מְאֹד *speaking Hebrew* (the action) *is very important*. Not all verbs form regular verbal nouns; in some their place is taken by other formations from the root, as מִשְׁלֹחַ *sending*, מַגָּע *touching* (from נגע), etc.

§ 76. The active participle is identical with the present tense of the active Binyanim and the passive participle with that of the passive Binyanim. Only the Kal has a special passive participle: כָּתוּב *written*.

§ 77. The imperative is identical with the corresponding forms of the future tense minus the prefixes. Differences in form are due to the rule that no Hebrew word can begin with two vowelless consonants or with a consonant that contained a strong Dagesh (§ 3 note). The imperative of *to write* is:

Masc. sing. כְּתֹב   Masc. pl. כִּתְבוּ
Fem. sing. כִּתְבִי   Fem. pl. כְּתֹבְנָה

Request is expressed by נָא after the imperative: בּוֹא נָא *come, please*.

§ 78. In conversation one often uses the future tense instead of the imperative, as this is felt to be less harsh. After בְּבַקָּשָׁה *please*, one employs mostly the infinitive: בְּבַקָּשָׁה לְהִכָּנֵס *please come in*.

Idiomatic Uses of Tenses

§ 79. Hebrew has only three tenses to express nearly all the shades of meaning which English represents by a much larger variety of compound forms. Thus כָּתַבְתִּי means: *I wrote, was writing, have written, had written, had been writing,* אֲנִי כּוֹתֵב *I write, am writing,* etc.

§ 80. The continuous past: *I have been writing* (and am still doing so), is rendered by the present tense, e.g. אֲנִי קוֹנֶה כָּאן זֶה כַּמָּה שָׁנִים *I have been buying here for several years,* כַּמָּה זְמָן אַתָּה בָּא״י? *how long have you been in Palestine?*

§ 81. Completed action, as in *I have written,* may if necessary be shown by prefixing כְּבָר (*already*): כְּבָר גָמַרְתִּי *I have finished.*

§ 82. There are various ways of differentiating shades of futurity, as אֲנִי עוֹמֵד לִכְתֹּב *I am about to write* and אֲנִי עָתִיד לִכְתֹּב *I am going to write,* סוֹפוֹ לָבוֹא הֵנָה *he is going to come here one day.* Colloquially one also says, אֲנִי הוֹלֵךְ· לִכְתֹּב *I am going to write.*

§ 83. The participle with the past of *to be,* הָיִיתִי כּוֹתֵב, etc., has two distinct meanings: (*a*) *I used to write,* e.g. הָיִינוּ הוֹלְכִים לְשָׁם כָּל יוֹם *we used to go there every day;* (*b*) *I would write* or *I would have written,* e.g. הָיִינוּ שְׂמֵחִים לִרְאוֹת אוֹתְךָ *we would be pleased to see you,* מִי הָיָה עוֹשֶׂה אַחֶרֶת? *who would have acted otherwise?* This form is mainly employed in hypothetical conditional clauses; see § 125.

§ 84. Progressive action is expressed with the help of לָלֶכֶת *to go:* אֶרֶץ יִשְׂרָאֵל הוֹלֶכֶת וְנִבְנֵית *Palestine is being built up more and more, is continually being built up.* This form must not be used for the English *to continue* with active verbs, as *we continue to build up Palestine,* which is אֲנַחְנוּ מַמְשִׁיכִים לִבְנוֹת אֶת א״י.

§ 85. In higher literary, and especially in poetic style, the future tense is often used for the present.

§ 86. The higher forms of literary style also employ some biblical constructions:

(*a*) The future tense (in some verbs with variations of form) with -וְ to express the past tense, as וַיֵּלֶךְ *and he went*, וַיָּקָם (**va-yakom**) *and he rose*. This form often implies that the event took place unexpectedly.

(*b*) The past tense with -וְ and the stress on the last syllable in all forms to denote a very certain future: וְהָלַכְתִּי *and then I shall go*.

(*c*) The absolute infinitive prefixed to the regular verbal form, as הָלוֹךְ אֵלֵךְ, הָלוֹךְ הָלַכְתִּי. This is simply a more solemn way of speaking.

§ 87. In a few idiomatic expressions, the present participle and the pronoun אֲנִי have become one word: חוֹשְׁבַנִי *methinks*, כִּמְדֻמַּנִי, דוֹמַנִי *it seems to me*, מְסֻפְּקַנִי *I doubt*, מֻבְטָחַנִי *I am sure*, זְכוּרַנִי *I remember*. The feminine is formed by inserting a ת before the -ני: חוֹשְׁבַתְנִי, etc.

The Binyanim

§ 88. The part of the verb to which prefixes and suffixes are joined is called the stem. This is made up from the consonants or root-letters (כ, ת, ב) by the addition of vowels, prefixes, and in some cases Dageshes, just like the pattern of the noun.

The formation of the past and future stems, as well as that of the present participle, imperative, infinitive, and verbal noun, obeys a number of schemes, four active and three passive, which are called Binyanim (*buildings*). These are named, like the noun-patterns, by substituting the root פעל for the third singular masculine of the past tense. Only the first, or simple, Binyan has a name, *The Light One*, meaning that no additions are made in it to the root.

Active	Passive
Kal	Nif'al
Pi'el	Pu'al
Hif'il	Hof'al
Hitpa'el	—

The following table shows these Binyanim from the root קבל.

THE BINYANIM OF קבל

NIF'AL	PI'EL	PU'AL	HIF'IL	HOF'AL	HITPA'EL

PAST

נִקְבַּלְתִּי	קִבַּלְתִּי	קֻבַּלְתִּי	הִקְבַּלְתִּי	הָקְבַּלְתִּי[1]	הִתְקַבַּלְתִּי
נִקְבַּלְתָּ	קִבַּלְתָּ	קֻבַּלְתָּ	הִקְבַּלְתָּ	הָקְבַּלְתָּ	הִתְקַבַּלְתָּ
נִקְבַּלְתְּ	קִבַּלְתְּ	קֻבַּלְתְּ	הִקְבַּלְתְּ	הָקְבַּלְתְּ	הִתְקַבַּלְתְּ
נִקְבַּל	קִבֵּל	קֻבַּל	הִקְבִּיל	הָקְבַּל	הִתְקַבֵּל
נִקְבְּלָה	קִבְּלָה	קֻבְּלָה	הִקְבִּילָה	הָקְבְּלָה	הִתְקַבְּלָה
נִקְבַּלְנוּ	קִבַּלְנוּ	קֻבַּלְנוּ	הִקְבַּלְנוּ	הָקְבַּלְנוּ	הִתְקַבַּלְנוּ
נִקְבַּלְתֶּם	קִבַּלְתֶּם	קֻבַּלְתֶּם	הִקְבַּלְתֶּם	הָקְבַּלְתֶּם	הִתְקַבַּלְתֶּם
נִקְבַּלְתֶּן	קִבַּלְתֶּן	קֻבַּלְתֶּן	הִקְבַּלְתֶּן	הָקְבַּלְתֶּן	הִתְקַבַּלְתֶּן
נִקְבְּלוּ	קִבְּלוּ	קֻבְּלוּ	הִקְבִּילוּ	הָקְבְּלוּ	הִתְקַבְּלוּ

FUTURE

אֶקָּבֵל	אֲקַבֵּל	אֲקֻבַּל	אַקְבִּיל	אָקְבַּל[1]	אֶתְקַבֵּל
תִּקָּבֵל	תְּקַבֵּל	תְּקֻבַּל	תַּקְבִּיל	תָּקְבַּל	תִּתְקַבֵּל
תִּקָּבְלִי	תְּקַבְּלִי	תְּקֻבְּלִי	תַּקְבִּילִי	תָּקְבְּלִי	תִּתְקַבְּלִי
יִקָּבֵל	יְקַבֵּל	יְקֻבַּל	יַקְבִּיל	יָקְבַּל	יִתְקַבֵּל
תִּקָּבֵל	תְּקַבֵּל	תְּקֻבַּל	תַּקְבִּיל	תָּקְבַּל	תִּתְקַבֵּל
נִקָּבֵל	נְקַבֵּל	נְקֻבַּל	נַקְבִּיל	נָקְבַּל	נִתְקַבֵּל
תִּקָּבְלוּ	תְּקַבְּלוּ	תְּקֻבְּלוּ	תַּקְבִּילוּ	תָּקְבְּלוּ	תִּתְקַבְּלוּ
תִּקָּבַלְנָה	תְּקַבֵּלְנָה	תְּקֻבַּלְנָה	תַּקְבֵּלְנָה	תָּקְבַּלְנָה	תִּתְקַבֵּלְנָה
יְקַבְּלוּ	יְקֻבְּלוּ	יַקְבִּילוּ	יָקְבְּלוּ	יִתְקַבְּלוּ	יִקָּבְלוּ
תִּקָּבַלְנָה	תְּקַבֵּלְנָה	תְּקֻבַּלְנָה	תַּקְבֵּלְנָה	תָּקְבַּלְנָה	תִּתְקַבֵּלְנָה

[1] Pronounce hokbalti, okbal, etc.

NIF'AL	PI'EL	PU'AL	HIF'IL	HOF'AL	HITPA'EL

PRESENT PARTICIPLE

נִקְבָּל	מְקַבֵּל	מְקֻבָּל	מַקְבִּיל	מָקְבָּל[1]	מִתְקַבֵּל
נִקְבָּלָה	מְקַבֶּלֶת	מְקֻבֶּלֶת	מַקְבִּילָה	מָקְבֶּלֶת	מִתְקַבֶּלֶת
נִקְבָּלִים	מְקַבְּלִים	מְקֻבָּלִים	מַקְבִּילִים	מָקְבָּלִים	מִתְקַבְּלִים
נִקְבָּלוֹת	מְקַבְּלוֹת	מְקֻבָּלוֹת	מַקְבִּילוֹת	מָקְבָּלוֹת	מִתְקַבְּלוֹת

IMPERATIVE

הִקָּבֵל	קַבֵּל	—	הַקְבֵּל	—	הִתְקַבֵּל
הִקָּבְלִי	קַבְּלִי	—	הַקְבִּילִי	—	הִתְקַבְּלִי
הִקָּבְלוּ	קַבְּלוּ	—	הַקְבִּילוּ	—	הִתְקַבְּלוּ
הִקָּבַלְנָה	קַבֵּלְנָה	—	הַקְבֵּלְנָה	—	הִתְקַבֵּלְנָה

INFINITIVE

| לְהִקָּבֵל | לְקַבֵּל | — | לְהַקְבִּיל | — | לְהִתְקַבֵּל |

VERBAL NOUN

| הִקָּבְלוּת | קַבּוּל | — | הַקְבָּלָה | — | הִתְקַבְּלוּת |

§ 89. In every verb we have therefore to consider (a) the root, (b) after which Binyan it is conjugated, (c) the meaning. Several verbs can be derived from one root according to different Binyanim, as on the opposite page: קָבַל *he complained*, קִבֵּל *he received*, הִקְבִּיל *he co-ordinated*, הִתְקַבֵּל *he was accepted*. On the other hand, the composition of the root radically affects the form of the Binyan, see § 95 ff.

The Binyanim also carry to some extent an element of meaning. There is no clear difference between the meaning of verbs in the Kal and such in the Pi'el. Mostly, when verbs of both Binyanim exist from one and the same root, they represent completely different root-meanings, as in קבל above.

---

[1] Pronounce **mokbal**, etc.

In a very few cases, the Pi'el denotes a more intensive form of action, as in שָׁבַר *he broke*, שִׁבֵּר *he smashed*, קָפַץ *he jumped*, קִפֵּץ *he jumped about*. The Pi'el is often used to derive verbs from nouns, as עִשֵּׁן *he smoked* from עָשָׁן *smoke*.

The Hif'il often denotes causative action, as הִכְתִּיב *he caused to write, dictated*, הִרְחִיב *he made wide, enlarged*, הֵנִיחַ *he caused to rest, put down*. There are, however, many verbs in this Binyan whose meaning is in no way causative, as הִשְׁמִין *he became fat*, הִרְגִּישׁ *he felt*.

The Hitpa'el often expresses reflexive action, as הִתְרַחֵץ *he washed himself*, הִתְנַצֵּל *he excused himself*, or reciprocal action as הִתְנַשְּׁקוּ *they kissed each other*, הִתְאַגְרְפוּ *they boxed with each other*, הִתְכַּתְּבוּ *they stood in correspondence*. Exceptions to these meanings, as לְהִתְפַּלֵּל *to pray*, are frequent, as in the Hif'il. While the meanings given here help one to guess at, and to remember the meaning of a verb, it must in each case be confirmed from the dictionary, just as only the dictionary will tell us which of the Binyanim exist of any root.

The Nif'al, while generally a passive to the Kal, also forms some verbs which are not passive and have no corresponding Kal-verbs, as נִלְחַם *he fought*, נִרְדַּם *he fell asleep*. Pu'al and Hof'al serve only as passives to Pi'el and Hif'al respectively.

Mixed Verbs

§ 90. A few verbs go in the past tense after one Binyan and in the future, present, and other forms after another Binyan, e.g. פָּחַדְתִּי *I was afraid* (Kal), but אֲנִי מְפַחֵד, אֶפְחַד, לְפַחֵד (Pi'el); or נָשַׁקְתִּי *I kissed* (Kal), future אֶשַּׁק or אֲנַשֵּׁק, present לְנַשֵּׁק, אֲנִי מְנַשֵּׁק. Also נִגַּשְׁתִּי *I approached* (Nif'al), present אֲנִי נִגָּשׁ, but אֶגַּשׁ, infinitive לָגֶשֶׁת (Kal). Similarly נֶהֱנֵיתִי *I enjoyed*, present אֲנִי נֶהֱנֶה (Nif'al), אָהֱנֶה, לֵהָנוֹת (Kal).

The Passives

§ 91. Many verbs in the Pi'el and Hif'il have besides their regular passives another in the Hitpa'el, which in this case mostly takes the form נִתְפַּעֵל in the past tense. Often there is a slight difference in meaning, e.g. לְבַקֵּשׁ *to request, to seek*: הַדָּבָר הַמְבֻקָּשׁ *the thing sought,* הַקָּהָל מִתְבַּקֵּשׁ *the public are requested,* הִרְחִיב *he enlarged,* הֻרְחַב or נִתְרַחֵב *it was enlarged* (but הִתְרַחֵב *it enlarged itself*).

§ 92. In the past and future tenses of the passive, Hebrew has separate forms to distinguish complete and continuous action. The first is expressed by the participle (in the case of the Nif'al, the פָּעוּל form) with the verb *to be*, the latter by the ordinary passive tenses, e.g. הַמִּכְתָּב הָיָה כָּתוּב עִבְרִית *the letter was written in Hebrew* (it is the completed letter that interests us), but הַמִּכְתָּב נִכְתַּב אֶתְמוֹל *the letter was written yesterday* (the action of writing took place yesterday). In the Nif'al, and in those verbs treated in § 91, the same distinction is observed in the present tense; the פָּעוּל form, the Pu'al and Hof'al participles are being used for the complete form, and the Nif'al and Hitpa'el participles for the continuous form.

§ 93. *By* with the passive is עַל יְדֵי. When the originator of the action is not mentioned, Hebrew often employs not the passive, but the active in the indefinite person (French *on*, German *man*), identical with the third plural masculine without the personal pronoun: מַכִּירִים אוֹתִי *I am known,* סִפְּרוּ לִי *I was told,* אֵיךְ אוֹמְרִים זֹאת בְּעִבְרִית? *how does one say this in Hebrew?* This construction must always be employed for the passive with verbs that do not take a person as direct object, as נָתְנוּ לִי *I was given,* יוֹדוּ לְךָ *you will be thanked,* טִפְּלוּ בּוֹ *he was looked after.*

§ 94. On the other hand, in some English verbs the active is used whether the subject is actually the originator or the object of the action, as *I open the door* and *the door opens*. Hebrew always employs the passive when the latter meaning is intended: הַדֶּלֶת נִפְתַּחַת *the door opens,* הָהַצָּגָה נִגְמְרָה *the performance ended,* הַסֵּפֶר נִמְכָּר הַרְבֵּה *the book sells well.*

Various Types of Roots

§ 95. The actual forms a verb takes in the different Binyanim are determined mainly by the letters of which the root is composed. If it contains one or more of the letters א, ה, ח, ע, ר (the laryngals), נ, ו, or י, the verbs derived from it will be different in their conjugation from the strong verbs like קבל, כתב.

Roots are described by relating the weak letters in them to the corresponding letters of פָּעַל, e.g. פ״נ is a verb whose first root-letter is נ, ע״ו one whose second root-letter is ו, etc. Roots with laryngals are referred to as 'lst lar.', etc.

§ 96. Generally speaking, all roots containing the same weak letter are conjugated in the same manner, so that by looking at the root one can decide which model it follows. Only in the Kal (and with פ״י in the Hif'il) are there differences within the same class of roots. But as some roots contain two weak letters, and their conjugation is influenced by both, as לְהַכּוֹת *to beat,* from נכה, and ירה *to shoot,* and there exist in the Kal a few entirely irregular verbs, it takes a good deal of experience to get all verbs right. The following paragraph shows the principal forms of all the more important varieties of verbal conjugation. The other forms of the verbs given can easily be derived from these. The table should be used in conjunction with the notes in § 98.

NOTE. In roots beginning with ס, שׂ, שׁ, the ת of the Hitpa'el changes places with the first root-letter: לְהִשְׁתַּמֵּשׁ *to use,* לְהִסְתַּכֵּל *to look.* If the root begins with ז or צ, not only do ת and the first root-letter change places, but with ז the ת becomes ד, and with צ it becomes ט: לְהִזְדָּרֵז *to hurry,* לְהִצְטַעֵר *to be sorry.* In roots beginning with ת, ד, ט, the ת is assimilated to the first root-letter, but this rule is often neglected to-day: לְהִתְדַּבֵּר or לְהִדַּבֵּר *to talk things over.*

48

§ 97.

KAL

	Past, 1st sg.	Past, 3rd sg.	Future	Imperative	Present	Infinitive	Verbal Noun	
1. Strong	כָּתַבְתִּי	כָּתַב	יִכְתֹּב	כְּתֹב	כּוֹתֵב	לִכְתֹּב	כְּתִיבָה	to write
2. ,,	שָׁכַבְתִּי	שָׁכַב	יִשְׁכַּב	שְׁכַב	שׁוֹכֵב	לִשְׁכַּב	שְׁכִיבָה	to lie down
3. ,,	כָּבַדְתִּי	כָּבֵד	יִכְבַּד	כְּבַד	כָּבֵד	לִכְבֹּד	—	to be heavy
4. 1st lar.	אָסַפְתִּי	אָסַף	יֶאֱסֹף	אֱסֹף	אוֹסֵף	לֶאֱסֹף	אֲסִיפָה	to collect
5. ,,	הָרַגְתִּי	הָרַג	יַהֲרֹג	הֲרֹג	הוֹרֵג	לַהֲרֹג	הֲרִיגָה	to kill
6. ,,	חָדַרְתִּי	חָדַר	יַחְדֹּר	חֲדֹר	חוֹדֵר	לַחְדֹּר	חֲדִירָה	to penetrate
7. א״פ	אָמַרְתִּי	אָמַר	יֹאמַר	אֱמֹר	אוֹמֵר	לֵאמֹר	אֲמִירָה	to say
8. נ״פ	נָפַלְתִּי	נָפַל	יִפֹּל	פֹּל	נוֹפֵל	לִפֹּל	נְפִילָה	to fall
9. ,,	נָגַעְתִּי	נָגַע	יִגַּע	גַּע	נוֹגֵעַ	לָגַעַת	נְגִיעָה	to touch
10. Irreg.	נָתַתִּי	נָתַן	יִתֵּן	תֵּן	נוֹתֵן	לָתֵת	נְתִינָה	to give
11. ,,	לָקַחְתִּי	לָקַח	יִקַּח	קַח	לוֹקֵחַ	לָקַחַת	לְקִיחָה	to take
12. פ״י	יָרַשְׁתִּי	יָרַשׁ	יִירַשׁ	יְרַשׁ	יוֹרֵשׁ	לִירֹשׁ	—	to inherit
13. ,,	יָשַׁנְתִּי	יָשֵׁן	יִישַׁן	יְשַׁן	יָשֵׁן	לִישֹׁן	יְשֵׁנָה	to sleep
14. ,,	יָשַׁבְתִּי	יָשַׁב	יֵשֵׁב	שֵׁב	יוֹשֵׁב	לָשֶׁבֶת	יְשִׁיבָה	to sit
15. ל״ה+פ״י	יָצָאתִי	יָצָא	יֵצֵא	צֵא	יוֹצֵא	לָצֵאת	יְצִיאָה	to go out
16. פ״י	יָצַקְתִּי	יָצַק	יִצֹּק	צֹק	יוֹצֵק	לָצֶקֶת	יְצִיקָה	to pour
17. Irreg.	יָכֹלְתִּי	יָכֹל	יוּכַל	—	יָכֹל	—	(יְכֹלֶת)	to be able
18. ,,	הָלַכְתִּי	הָלַךְ	יֵלֵךְ	לֵךְ	הוֹלֵךְ	לָלֶכֶת	הֲלִיכָה	to go

49

KAL (continued)

	Past, 1st sg.	Past, 3rd sg.	Future	Imperative	Present	Infinitive	Verbal Noun	
19. ע"ו	שַׁבְתִּי	שָׁב	יָשׁוּב	שׁוּב	שָׁב	לָשׁוּב	שִׁיבָה	to return
20. ,,	שַׁרְתִּי	שָׁר	יָשִׁיר	שִׁיר	שָׁר	לָשִׁיר	שִׁירָה	to sing
21. ,,	בָּאתִי	בָּא	יָבוֹא	בּוֹא	בָּא	לָבוֹא	בִּיאָה	to come
22. ,,	מַתִּי	מֵת	יָמוּת	מוּת	מֵת	לָמוּת	מִיתָה	to die
23. ל"א	שָׂנֵאתִי	שָׂנֵא	יִשְׂנָא	שְׂנָא	שׂוֹנֵא	לִשְׂנֹא	(שִׂנְאָה)	to hate
24. ל"ה	קָנִיתִי	קָנָה	יִקְנֶה	קְנֵה	קוֹנֶה	לִקְנוֹת	קְנִיָּה	to buy
25. ,, + 1st lar.	עָשִׂיתִי	עָשָׂה (עֲשָׂתָה)	יַעֲשֶׂה (תַּעֲשִׂי)	עֲשֵׂה	עוֹשֶׂה	לַעֲשׂוֹת	עֲשִׂיָּה	to do
26. ע"ע	סַבֹּתִי	סַב	יָסֹב	סֹב	סוֹבֵב	לָסֹב	—	to go round

NIF'AL

27. Strong	נִכְנַסְתִּי	נִכְנַס	יִכָּנֵס	הִכָּנֵס	נִכְנָס	לְהִכָּנֵס	—	to enter
28. 1st lar.	נֶעֱלַמְתִּי	נֶעֱלַם	יֵעָלֵם	הֵעָלֵם	נֶעֱלָם	לְהֵעָלֵם (לְהֵעָלֵם)	—	to disappear
29. ג"ר	נִזּוֹקְתִּי	נִזּוֹק	יִזּוֹק	הִזּוֹק	נִזּוֹק	לְהִזּוֹק	—	to be damaged
30. ל"י	נִפְזַרְתִּי	נִפְזַר	יִפָּזֵר	הִפָּזֵר	נִפְזָר	לְהִפָּזֵר	—	to be scattered
31. פ"י	נוֹלַדְתִּי	נוֹלַד	יִוָּלֵד	הִוָּלֵד	נוֹלָד	לְהִוָּלֵד	—	to be born
32. ל"א	נִקְרֵאתִי	נִקְרָא	אֶקָּרֵא	הִקָּרֵא	נִקְרָא	לְהִקָּרֵא	—	to be called
33. ל"ה	נִקְנֵיתִי	נִקְנָה (נִקְנְתָה)	יִקָּנֶה (תִּקָּנֶה)	הִקָּנֶה	נִקְנֶה	לְהִקָּנוֹת	—	to be bought
34. ,,							—	to become
35. ע"ע							—	to melt

50

PI'EL

36. Strong	קִבַּלְתִּי	קִבֵּל	יְקַבֵּל	קַבֵּל	מְקַבֵּל	קַבֵּל to receive
37. 2nd lar.	בֵּאַרְתִּי	בֵּאֵר	יְבָאֵר	בָּאֵר	מְבָאֵר	בֵּאֵר to explain
38. פ״י	קִיַּמְתִּי	קִיֵּם	יְקַיֵּם	קַיֵּם	מְקַיֵּם	קִיֵּם to fulfil
39. ,,	רוֹמַמְתִּי	רוֹמֵם	יְרוֹמֵם	רוֹמֵם	מְרוֹמֵם	— to raise
40. א״ל	בִּטַּאתִי	בַּטֵּא	יְבַטֵּא	בַּטֵּא	מְבַטֵּא	בִּטֵּא to pronounce
41. ה״ל	שִׁנִּיתִי	שִׁנָּה (שַׁנּוֹת)	יְשַׁנֶּה	שַׁנֵּה	מְשַׁנֶּה	שִׁנָּה to alter
42. ע״ע	סִבַּבְתִּי	סִבֵּב	יְסַבֵּב	סַבֵּב	מְסַבֵּב	סִבֵּב to turn
43. 4 letters	פִּרְסַמְתִּי	פִּרְסֵם	יְפַרְסֵם	פַּרְסֵם	מְפַרְסֵם	פִּרְסֵם to publish

PU'AL

36a. Strong	קֻבַּלְתִּי	קֻבַּל	יְקֻבַּל	מְקֻבָּל	(מְקֻבָּלִי)	— to be received
37a. 2nd lar.	בֹּאַרְתִּי	בֹּאַר	יְבֹאַר	מְבֹאָר	—	— to be explained
38a. פ״י	קֻיַּמְתִּי	קֻיַּם	יְקֻיַּם	מְקֻיָּם	—	— to be fulfilled
39a. ,,	רוֹמַמְתִּי	רוֹמַם	יְרוֹמַם	מְרוֹמָם	—	— to be raised
40a. ל״א	בֻּטֵּאתִי	בֻּטָּא	יְבֻטָּא	מְבֻטָּא	—	— to be pronounced
41a. ה״ל	שֻׁנֵּיתִי	שֻׁנָּה	יְשֻׁנֶּה	מְשֻׁנֶּה	—	— to be altered
42a. ע״ע	סֻבַּבְתִּי	סֻבַּב	יְסֻבַּב	מְסֻבָּב	—	— to be turned
43a. 4 letters	פֻּרְסַמְתִּי	פֻּרְסַם	יְפֻרְסַם	מְפֻרְסָם	—	— to be published

HIF'IL

	Past, 1st sg.	Past, 3rd sg.	Future	Imperative	Present	Infinitive	Verbal Noun	
44. Strong	הִכְתַּבְתִּי	הִכְתִּיב	יַכְתִּיב	הַכְתֵּב	מַכְתִּיב	לְהַכְתִּיב	הַכְתָּבָה	to dictate
45. 1st lar.	הֶחֱלַפְתִּי	הֶחֱלִיף	יַחֲלִיף	הַחֲלֵף	מַחֲלִיף	לְהַחֲלִיף	הַחְלָפָה	to change
46. פ"נ	הֵיטַבְתִּי	הֵיטִיב	יֵיטִיב	הֵיטֵב	מֵיטִיב	לְהֵיטִיב	הֲטָבָה	to make good
47. ,,	הוֹשַׁבְתִּי	הוֹשִׁיב	יוֹשִׁיב	הוֹשֵׁב	מוֹשִׁיב	לְהוֹשִׁיב	הוֹשָׁבָה	to make sit
48. פ"י or ע"י	הִצַּגְתִּי	הִצִּיג	יַצִּיג	הַצֵּג	מַצִּיג	לְהַצִּיג	הַצָּגָה	to represent
49. ע"ו	הֵסַרְתִּי	הֵסִיר	יָסִיר	הָסֵר	מֵסִיר	לְהָסִיר	הֲסָרָה	to take off
50. ,,	הֵבֵאתִי	הֵבִיא	יָבִיא	הָבֵא	מֵבִיא	לְהָבִיא	הֲבָאָה	to bring
51. ל"ה	הִשְׁקֵיתִי	הִשְׁקָה	יַשְׁקֶה	הַשְׁקֵה	מַשְׁקֶה	לְהַשְׁקוֹת	הַשְׁקָיָה	to water
52. ל"ה+פ"י	הוֹרֵיתִי	הוֹרָה	יוֹרֶה	הוֹרֵה	מוֹרֶה	לְהוֹרוֹת	הוֹרָאָה	to teach
53. ל"ה+ע"י	הִכֵּיתִי	הִכָּה	יַכֶּה	הַכֵּה	מַכֶּה	לְהַכּוֹת	הַכָּאָה	to beat
54. ע"ע	הֵקַלּוֹתִי	הֵקֵל	יָקֵל	הָקֵל	מֵקֵל	לְהָקֵל	הֲקָלָה	to make easy

HOF'AL

	Past, 1st sg.[1]	Past, 3rd sg.	Future	Imperative	Present	Infinitive	Verbal Noun	
44a. Strong	הֻכְתַּבְתִּי	הֻכְתַּב	יֻכְתַּב	—	מֻכְתָּב	(לְהֻכְתַּב)	—	to be dictated
45a. 1st lar.	הָחְלַפְתִּי	הָחְלַף	יָחְלַף	—	מָחְלָף	—	—	to be changed

46a, 47a. פ״י	הוּשַׁבְתִּי,	הוּשַׁב	יֻשַׁב	—	מוּשָׁב	—	to be made to sit
48a. פ״נ or פ״י	הֻצַּגְתִּי,	הֻצַּג	יֻצַּג	—	מֻצָּג	—	to be represented
49a. ע״ו	הוּסַר	הוּסַר	יוּסַר	—	מוּסָר	—	to be taken off
50a. ,,	הוּבָאתִי,	הוּבָא	יוּבָא	—	מוּבָא	—	to be brought
51a. ל״ה	הֻשְׁקֵיתִי,	הֻשְׁקָה	יֻשְׁקֶה	—	מֻשְׁקֶה	—	to be watered
52a. ל״ה+פ״י	הוּרֵיתִי,	הוּרָה	יוּרֶה	—	מוּרֶה	—	to be taught
53a. ל״ה+פ״נ	הֻכֵּיתִי	הֻכָּה	יֻכֶּה	—	מֻכֶּה	—	to be beaten
54a. ע״ע	הוּקַלּוֹתִי,	הוּקַל	יֻקַל	—	מוּקָל	—	to be made easy

HITPA‛EL

55. Strong	הִתְגַּבַּרְתִּי,	הִתְגַּבֵּר	יִתְגַּבֵּר	מִתְגַּבֵּר	לְהִתְגַּבֵּר	הִתְגַּבְּרוּת	to overcome
56. פ״י	הִתְיַצַּבְתִּי	הִתְיַצֵּב	יִתְיַצֵּב	מִתְיַצֵּב	לְהִתְיַצֵּב	הִתְיַצְּבוּת	to take place
57. פ״י or ע״ע	הִתְקוֹמַמְתִּי,	הִתְקוֹמֵם	יִתְקוֹמֵם	מִתְקוֹמֵם	לְהִתְקוֹמֵם	הִתְקוֹמְמוּת	to rebel
58. א״ל	הִתְרַפֵּאתִי,	הִתְרַפֵּא	יִתְרַפֵּא	מִתְרַפֵּא	לְהִתְרַפֵּא	הִתְרַפְּאוּת	to cure oneself
59. ל״ה	הִתְכַּסֵּיתִי,	הִתְכַּסָּה	יִתְכַּסֶּה	מִתְכַּסֶּה	לְהִתְכַּסּוֹת	הִתְכַּסּוּת	to cover oneself
60. 4 letters	הִשְׁתַּפַּרְנַסְתִּי,	הִשְׁתַּפַּרְנֵס	יִשְׁתַּפַּרְנֵס	מִשְׁתַּפַּרְנֵס	לְהִשְׁתַּפַּרְנֵס	הִשְׁתַּפַּרְנְסוּת	to make a living

[1] Pronounce hoch̲tavti and so in all other Hof‛al forms.

Notes to the Paradigms

No. 3. So לִרְעֹב *to be hungry*, לַעֲרֹב *to be pleasant, to guarantee*, etc.

Nos. 4–6. Verbs beginning with א like 4 (but see 7), those beginning with ה or ע like 5, those beginning with ח like 6. Verbs with ר are strong.

No. 7. So לֶאֱהֹב *to love*, לֶאֱחֹז *to seize*, לֶאֱבֹד *to be lost*.

Nos. 8, 29. So all verbs beginning with נ except those in which the second root-letter is א, ה, ח, ע, as לִנְאֹם *to speak*, לִנְחֹר *to snore*. נ is also preserved in לִנְבֹּחַ *to bark*.

No. 12. So all verbs beginning with י, except the following: יבשׁ *to be dry*, יעף *to be tired*, ירא (יְרֵאתִי) *to fear*, go like no. 13. ילד *to bear a child*, ירד *to descend*, go like no. 14. ידע *to know* is יֵדַע, etc. in the future.

No. 16. So also יצר *to create*.

No. 20. In all other Binyanim roots ע"י are conjugated like ע"ו.

No. 23. So מלא *to be full*, and (in the past) ירא *to fear* (in the future no. 13). Other verbs ל"א are strong, but have ָ for ַ in all forms.

No. 26. The name ע"ע denotes verbs in which the second and third root-letters are equal. Past tense also סַבֹּתָ, סַבֹּתִי, etc.

Nos. 38, 55. So לְמֵין *to classify*, לְעֵיֵן *to glance*, לְצַיֵּר *to paint*, etc., but most ע"ו verbs follow no. 39.

No. 42. In Pi'el, Pu'al and Hitpa'el, ע"ע verbs follow the ע"ו.

No. 43. Verbs with four and five root-letters are only conjugated in the Pi'el, Pu'al and Hitpa'el.

No. 48. Of פ"י roots only those with a צ as second root-letter (of which לְהַצִּיג is one). All פ"נ verbs except those with א, ה, ח, ע as second root-letter.

No. 49. In the past also הֲסִירֹת, הֲסִירֹתִי, etc.

Idiomatic Constructions

§ 98. 'To be'

In the past and future tenses, *to be* is לִהְיוֹת (like לִקְנוֹת no. 24).

54

In the present tense, *to be* is not expressed at all: הָעִיר גְדוֹלָה *the town is large,* הַמַּיִם בַּבַּקְבּוּק *the water is in the bottle,* מִי שָׁם? *who is there?*

§ 99. To make the construction clearer, הוא (or הִיא, etc., as required) may be inserted, and must be, if there is any danger of ambiguity, e.g. יִצְחָק הַקָּטָן may mean *little Isaac* or *Isaac is the little one,* but יִצְחָק הוּא הַקָּטָן has definitely the second meaning. Generally, הוא must be inserted when both subject and predicate have the article, or when the subject consists in a long string of words.

§ 100. The negative of *to be* in the present tense is אֵין with suffix pronouns. For אֵינִי, אֵינוֹ, אֵינָהּ one can also say אֵינֶנִּי, אֵינֶנּוּ, אֵינֶנָּה, e.g. אֵינֶנּוּ כָּאן *he is not here,* הַסְחוֹרָה אֵינָהּ טוֹבָה *the material is not good,* הַיֶּלֶד אֵינֶנּוּ *the child is not there.*

The same can be expressed by uninflected אֵין preceding the subject: אֵין הַדָּבָר כָּךְ *the matter is not so.*

§ 101. In colloquial style, לֹא is often used instead of אֵין, both when meaning *is not* and as negation of the present (see § 112). This is, however, still considered ungrammatical and should not be imitated.

§ 102. *There is* is יֵשׁ for all numbers and genders: יֵשׁ מַיִם בַּכַּד *there is water in the jug,* יֵשׁ כָּאן הַרְבֵּה אֲנָשִׁים *there are many people here.* In literary style, יֵשׁ may be omitted, but then the words denoting place must precede the subject: עַל הַשֻּׁלְחָן פְּרָחִים; בַּכַּד מַיִם *there are flowers on the table.* *There is not* is uninflected אֵין, e.g. אֵין כָּאן אִישׁ *there is no one here.*

§ 103. יֵשׁ also means *he (it) is present,* יֶשְׁנִי *I am present,* יֶשְׁנָהּ, יֶשְׁנוֹ, יֶשְׁךָ, etc.

§ 104. 'To have'

There is no verb *to have,* but one says *there is to me,* e.g. יֵשׁ לִי פְּנַאי *I have time,* אֵין לוֹ שֵׂכֶל *he has no sense.* The word which in English is object of *to have* is here the subject, and must not be preceded by אֶת.

In the past and future tenses, לִהְיוֹת is used for יֵשׁ. The form must agree in gender and number with the object possessed: הָיָה לוֹ בַּיִת *he had a house*, לֹא תִהְיֶה לְךָ הִזְדַּמְּנוּת *you won't have an opportunity*.

§ 105. 'Must'

I must is expressed in three different ways:

(a) By עַל with suffix pronouns: עָלַי לָלֶכֶת *I must go* (lit. *it is upon me to go*).

(b) By the impersonal phrases צָרִיךְ *it is necessary*, יֵשׁ *it is right*, מִן הָרָאוּי *it is proper*. צָרִיךְ לָלֶכֶת may mean, according to the context, *I must go, you must go*, etc.

(c) By צָרִיךְ constructed like a present tense: אֲנִי צָרִיךְ לָלֶכֶת.

The past and future tenses are made by placing הָיָה and יִהְיֶה in front of constructions (a) or (b), and the personal forms of לִהְיוֹת before (c): הָיִיתִי צָרִיךְ לָלֶכֶת, הָיָה עָלַי לָלֶכֶת, יִהְיֶה צָרִיךְ לָלֶכֶת. One can also use the construction for *to have*, e.g. הָיָה לְךָ לֹאמַר לוֹ *you had to tell him*.

§ 106. *I must not* is אָסוּר לִי (lit. *it is forbidden to me*): אָסוּר לְךָ לֹאמַר כָּךְ *you must not say so*. The same is also expressed by אַל לִי or אֵין לִי, e.g. אַל לָנוּ לְהִתְיָאֵשׁ *we must not despair*.

§ 107. 'To need'

I need something is expressed by various adjectival constructions: נָחוּץ לִי דָבָר (*I require it, want to have it*), אֲנִי זָקוּק לְדָבָר (*I possess it, but cannot do without it*), לִי דָבָר *I am in need of something*.

§ 108. *To need* with verbs is expressed by the various phrases for *must*, or by מְכֻרְחֲךָ *compelled*, אַתָּה מְכֻרְחֲךָ לָלֶכֶת עַכְשָׁו? *need you go now?* *I need not* is אֵין (לִי) צֹרֶךְ, e.g. אֵין צֹרֶךְ לְחַכּוֹת *oou need not wait*.

§ 109. 'To like'

I like something in the sense of 'I am pleased with it' is
הַדָּבָר מוֹצֵא חֵן בְּעֵינַי (lit. *it finds favour in my eyes*), e.g.
הַמַּחֲזֶה מָצָא חֵן בְּעֵינֵי כָּל אֶחָד *everyone liked the play very much.* But
like in the sense of 'to be fond of' is לֶאֱהֹב (*to love*): אַתָּה אוֹהֵב
שׁוֹקוֹלָדָה? *do you like chocolate?*, הִיא אוֹהֶבֶת לִקְרֹא *she likes to read.*
When it means no more than 'to want', it is rendered by
לִרְצוֹת: אַתָּה רוֹצֶה לָבוֹא מָחָר? *would you like to come to-morrow?*

§ 110. 'To be able'

I can is אֲנִי יָכֹל (§ 97, no. 17), but when speaking of an
acquired ability, one uses אֲנִי יוֹדֵעַ (*I know*), e.g. הִיא יוֹדַעַת לִרְקֹד
she can dance (הִיא יְכֹלָה לִרְקֹד would mean *she is in a fit state to
dance*). *I can* in the sense of *I succeed* is עוֹלֶה בְּיָדִי, e.g. לֹא עָלָה
בְּיָדִי לִמְצֹא אוֹתוֹ *I could not find him.*

§ 111.

Related to the idea of ability is the meaning of the
two verbs לְהַסְפִּיק and לִזְכּוֹת, both of which have no real
equivalent in English. לְהַסְפִּיק means *to manage, have time to,*
as הִסְפַּקְתִּי לִרְאוֹת אוֹתוֹ *I managed to see him,* לֹא הִסְפִּיקוּ לָצֵאת עַד
שֶׁרָאָה אוֹתָם *they did not have time to get out before he noticed
them.*

לִזְכּוֹת denotes that something happens through luck, as
מָתַי נִזְכֶּה לִרְאוֹת אוֹתְךָ? *when shall we see you?* cf. זָכָה בַּהַגְרָלָה *he
won in a lottery.*

Negation

§ 112.

The negation for the past and future tenses is לֹא
placed before the verb. The present tense is negated by the
negative forms of *to be* (§ 98): לֹא כָּתַבְתִּי, לֹא אֶכְתֹּב, but אֵינֶנִּי כּוֹתֵב,
אֵינְךָ כּוֹתֵב, etc.

The negative imperative is expressed by the future tense
with אַל e.g. אַל תֵּלֵךְ *don't go.*

§ 113.

Negative forms of nouns and adjectives are made
up by placing בִּלְתִּי and in some cases לֹא or אִי before the word:
אִי־נְעִימוּת *unusual,* בִּלְתִּי אֱנוֹשִׁי *inhuman,* לֹא־יְהוּדִי *non-Jew,* בִּלְתִּי רָגִיל

unpleasantness, אִי אֶפְשָׁר *it is impossible,* but בִּלְתִּי אֶפְשָׁרִי *impossible* (adjective); אַל־חוּט *wireless.*

The Object of the Verb

§ 114. If the direct object has the article, or is defined by a pronoun suffix, or by being a proper name, the particle אֵת is inserted before it: אֲנִי רוֹאֶה אֶת הַבַּיִת *I see the house,* רוֹאֶה אֶת בֵּיתְךָ *I see your house,* אֲנִי רוֹאֶה אֶת דָּוִד *I see David,* but if the object is undefined, it is not marked in any way: אֲנִי רוֹאֶה בַּיִת *I see a house.*

§ 115. When a pronoun is object to a verb, it must be in the suffix form: רְאִינוּךָ *we saw you,* יִרְאוּנִי *they will see me.* Both verbs and pronouns undergo considerable changes in that process.

Instead of directly to the verb, the pronouns can be suffixed to אוֹת- (אֵת=): יִרְאוּ אוֹתִי, רָאִינוּ אוֹתְךָ. This is the more usual construction in conversational style, and the only one possible with the present tense.

THE SENTENCE

§ 116. Order of Words

Normally the subject precedes the verb and the object follows it: אֲנִי רוֹאֶה אֶת הָעִיר *I see the town.* But when it is desired to stress a word, it can be put at the beginning of the sentence: אֶת הָעִיר אֲנִי רוֹאֶה *it is the town I see,* רוֹאֶה אֲנִי אֶת הָעִיר *I do see the town.*

The verb can be put before the subject also when no special stress is intended. It is usually placed first when the sentence opens with an adverbial phrase or a subordinate clause, e.g. בְּעוֹד שָׁבוּעַ יֵצֵא אָחִי לְחוּץ לָאָרֶץ *in a week's time my brother will go abroad,* כְּשֶׁנִּכְנַסְנוּ הִשְׁתּוֹמְמוּ כֻּלָּם *when we came in, everyone was astonished.*

§ 117. Questions

There is no alteration in the order of words. In conversation, questions are mostly distinguished only by their intonation. When it is desired to make it clearer that the sentence is meant as a question, ־הַ or הַאִם is put in front of it. כְּלוּם introduces a question to which the answer *no* is expected: כְּלוּם הָיִיתָ כָּאן? *you haven't been here, have you?* The English phrases *isn't it? didn't you?* etc. after sentences may be translated by לֹא כֵן? *is it not so?* but this is much less frequent in Hebrew than the expressions mentioned are in English.

§ 118. Indirect questions are introduced by אִם, e.g. שָׁאַל אוֹתִי אִם אָבוֹא *he asked me if I would come,* אֵינֶנִּי יוֹדֵעַ אִם בָּא *I don't know whether he has come.*

Subordinate Clauses

§ 119. The principal subordinating conjunction is ־שֶׁ *that* (in literary style also כִּי). It is employed wherever English has *that*, as in אֲנִי יוֹדֵעַ שֶׁהוּא כָּאן *I know that he is here*, and must not be left out even where *that* may be suppressed in English. It must also be used after verbs of wishing, etc., when the subject of the subordinate clause is different from that of the principal clause, e.g. אֲנִי רוֹצֶה לָלֶכֶת *I want to go*, but אֲנִי רוֹצֶה שֶׁתֵּלֵךְ *I want you to go.*

§ 120. The tenses of subordinate clauses are the same as they would have been if the clause had stood by itself. There is no 'sequence of tenses' as in English, e.g. when I say *He told me he was ill*, his actual words were 'I am ill', therefore the Hebrew is אָמַר לִי שֶׁהוּא חוֹלֶה. Similarly חָשַׁב שֶׁהָלְכָה *he thought that she had gone,* כָּתַב לִי שֶׁיָּבוֹא *he wrote me he would come.* After verbs of wishing, ordering, etc., the verb is in the future tense, because with reference to the main verb the (yet unfulfilled) action is future.

Conjunctions

§ 121. Most subordinating conjunctions are originally prepositions, and require ־שֶׁ or אֲשֶׁר to complete them. The following is a list of the most common co-ordinating and subordinating conjunctions:

after	אַחֲרֵי שֶׁ-	lest	שֶׁמָּא, פֶּן, לְבַל
also	גַם, אַף	or	אוֹ
although	אַף עַל פִּי שֶׁ-, אִם כִּי	in order that	כְּדֵי שֶׁ-, עַל מְנָת שֶׁ-
as if	כְּאִלוּ	since	מִזְּמַן שֶׁ-, מֵאָז, מִכֵּיוָן שֶׁ-
as long as	כָּל זְמַן שֶׁ-, כָּל עוֹד	so that	עַד שֶׁ-, כְּדֵי שֶׁ-
because	מִפְּנֵי שֶׁ-, הוֹאִיל וְ-, כִּי	unless	בִּלְתִי אִם, אִם לֹא, אֶלָּא אִם כֵּן
before	לִפְנֵי שֶׁ-, עַד שֶׁ-	until	עַד שֶׁ-
but	אֲבָל, אוּלָם, אֶלָּא (שֶׁ-)	when	כְּשֶׁ-, כַּאֲשֶׁר, כֵּיוָן שֶׁ-
if	אִם, לוּ	when (future)	לִכְשֶׁ-
in so far as	עַד כַּמָה שֶׁ-	while	בִּזְמַן שֶׁ-, בְּשָׁעָה שֶׁ-, כָּל עוֹד

§ 122. גַם is placed before the noun to which it refers: גַם הוּא בָּא *he, too, came,* רָאִיתִי גַם אוֹתָךְ *I saw you, too.* In the form גַם כֵּן it can be placed after the word to which it refers, or anywhere else in the sentence.

§ 123. *And* is -וְ. Before ב, ו, מ or פ, and before any consonant with -ְ, it becomes -וּ: וּבַיִת *and a house,* וּשְׂמִיכָה *and a blanket.* Before יְ it becomes -וִ, e.g. וִירוּשָׁלַיִם *and Jerusalem.*

Conditional Clauses

§ 124. For introducing conditions which may have been, or are likely to be, fulfilled, אִם is used, e.g. אִם אֵינְךָ יוֹדֵעַ, אֹמַר לְךָ *if you don't know, I will tell you.* If the condition is not yet fulfilled, the future tense must be used: אִם תִּרְאֶה אוֹתוֹ, דְּרשׁ בִּשְׁלוֹמוֹ *if you see him, give him my regards.*

§ 125. If it is known that the condition has not been fulfilled (hypothetical condition), לוּ, followed by the past tense, is used for אִם, while the principal clause has the present participle with הָיָה (see § 83), e.g. לוּ שָׁאַלְתָּ אוֹתִי, הָיִיתִי אוֹמֵר לְךָ *if you had asked me I would have told you.* The negative of this is לוּלֵא, e.g. לוּלֵא יָרַד גֶּשֶׁם הָיִינוּ הוֹלְכִים לְטַיֵּל *if it did not rain we might have gone for a walk.*

Relative Clauses

§ 126. The principles on which the Hebrew relative clause is constructed are quite different from those of the English one. In the sentence *the house in which I live*, we have a relative pronoun 'which' referring to the antecedent 'the house'. The relative pronoun itself is dependent on the preposition 'in' which precedes the whole relative clause. In Hebrew there is no relative pronoun. The relative clause is introduced by a particle -שֶׁ or אֲשֶׁר which merely introduces it. The pronoun referring to the antecedent follows the -שֶׁ, and any preposition which **precedes** the relative clause in English must come **within** it in Hebrew. The above sentence becomes therefore: הַבַּיִת שֶׁאֲנִי גָר בּוֹ lit. *the house—that—I live in it.* Similarly הַגְּבֶרֶת שֶׁדִּבַּרְתָּ עִמָּהּ *the lady to whom you were speaking*, הָאִישׁ שֶׁאֲנַחְנוּ נִמְצָאִים עַל אַדְמָתוֹ *the man on whose land we are*. The best way to get these clauses right is to imagine them as independent sentences: *the man—we are on his land*, etc.

§ 127. The relative adverbs *where*, etc. must be resolved into their elements, e.g. *the town where we were* becomes *the town in which we were*: הָעִיר שֶׁבָּהּ הָיִינוּ. Instead of the pronoun referring back one can in this case use שָׁם *there*: הָעִיר שֶׁשָּׁם הָיִינוּ (lit. *the town—which—we were there*).

§ 128. The pronoun referring back may be left out when it would be subject or direct object in the relative clause, e.g. הַסֵּפֶר שֶׁעַל הַשֻּׁלְחָן *the book which is on the table*, הַמְּקוֹמוֹת שֶׁרָאִיתִי *the places which I saw*.

§ 129. The relative particle must not be left out, as in the English *the places we saw*. Only in high literary style the particle may sometimes be omitted when the antecedent is without the definite article.

§ 130. When the verb of the relative clause is in the present tense, and its subject identical with the antecedent, the article is used instead of ‑שֶׁ: הָאִישׁ הַהוֹלֵךְ שָׁם *the man who goes there*, בַּשָּׁנָה הַבָּאָה *in the year which comes, next year*.[1] The construction is different from that of an adjective in so far as the participle may have the article even if the antecedent has none, e.g. אֲנָשִׁים הָרוֹצִים לִלְמֹד עִבְרִית *people who want to learn Hebrew*. But when the verb is negative, or when the subject is different from the antecedent, ‑שֶׁ must be used: הַחֲבֵרִים שֶׁאֵינָם נוֹכָחִים *the Chaverim who are not present*, הַסֵּפֶר שֶׁאֲנִי קוֹרֵא *the book which I am reading*.

SHORT PHRASES

שָׁלוֹם	Peace! (*the universal greeting formula*).
מַה שְׁלוֹמְךָ (‑ֵךְ)?	How are you?
טוֹב, תּוֹדָה	All right, thank you.
וּמַה שְׁלוֹמְךָ אַתָּה?	And how are you?
תּוֹדָה	Thank you.
תּוֹדָה רַבָּה	Many thanks.
עַל לֹא דָבָר	Not at all.
בְּבַקָּשָׁה	Please.
בְּבַקָּשָׁה לָשֶׁבֶת	Please sit down.
בְּרָצוֹן	With pleasure.
סְלִיחָה	Sorry.
אֵין דָּבָר	It's all right, never mind.
יִישַׁר כֹּחַךָ	Well done.
חֲבָל!	What a pity.
הִתְבַּיֵּשׁ	Shame on you.
בּוּז!	Shame!
תּוֹדָה לָאֵל	Thank God.

[1] But *last year* is בַּשָּׁנָה שֶׁעָבְרָה (*in the year which passed*).

אִם יִרְצֶה הַשֵּׁם	Please God.
מַזָל טוֹב	Congratulations.
בְּשָׁעָה טוֹבָה וּמֻצְלַחַת!	Best of luck.
בָּרוּךְ הַבָּא	Welcome.
יִבְסַם לְךָ, בְּתֵיאָבוֹן	Bon appétit.
לְחַיִּים	Your health!
תִּתְחַדֵּשׁ	Renew yourself (*said to someone who wears something new*).
טוֹב מְאֹד	Very well.
מְצֻיָן	Excellent.
לֹא יְאֻמַן כִּי יְסֻפַּר	Unbelievable!
בֹּקֶר טוֹב	Good morning.
שַׁבָּת שָׁלוֹם	Good Sabbath.
חַגִּים לְשִׂמְחָה	Happy festivals.
לְהִתְרָאוֹת	Good-bye.
לֵיל מְנוּחָה	Good-night.

1. בִּנְמַל תֵּל־אָבִיב

שִׁמְעוֹן וְרָחֵל נִשְׁעָנִים עַל מַעֲקֵה הָאֳנִיָה וּמַבִּיטִים אֶל הַחוֹף הַנִּרְאֶה מֵרָחוֹק. הָאֳנִיָה מִתְקָרֶבֶת לְאַט לְאַט אֶל הַנָּמֵל וְהַסִּירוֹת הָרִאשׁוֹנוֹת יוֹצְאוֹת לִקְרָאתָהּ.

רחל: אִם כֵּן, זֹאת הִיא אֶרֶץ־יִשְׂרָאֵל, אֶרֶץ חֲלוֹמוֹתַי! מִי הָיָה מְנַבֵּא[1] לִי שֶׁאֶזְכֶּה[2] כָּל כָּךְ מַהֵר לִרְאוֹת אוֹתָהּ!

שמעון: מִכָּל מָקוֹם אֵינֵךְ בָּאָה אֵלֶיהָ כְּזָרָה. מִתּוֹךְ דִּבּוּרֵךְ הָעִבְרִי אִישׁ לֹא הָיָה מַכִּיר בָּךְ שֶׁאֵינֵךְ "צַבְּרָה"[3]. הֲרֵי[4] אַתְּ כְּבָר אֶרֶץ־יִשְׂרְאֵלִית לַמֶּחֱצָה.

רחל: אַתָּה טוֹעֶה, אֲהוּבִי. זֶה שְׁבוּעַיִם, מִזְמַן שֶׁנִּשֵּׂאתִי לְךָ, אֲנִי אֶרֶץ יִשְׂרְאֵלִית גְּמוּרָה. אֲבָל בֶּאֱמֶת, שֶׁהָיִיתִי בָּאָרֶץ הַזֹּאת כָּל כָּךְ הַרְבֵּה בְּמַחְשְׁבוֹתַי שֶׁאֲנִי מַרְגִּישָׁה כְּאִלּוּ אֲנִי שָׁבָה אֵלֶיהָ. וּבְכָל זֹאת, אֵינִי יְכוֹלָה לְהִמָּנַע מֵחֲשָׁשׁ יָדוּעַ. הַאִם אֶמְצָא אֶת הָאָרֶץ הַזֹּאת כְּמוֹ שֶׁתֵּאַרְתִּי לִי אוֹתָהּ, אוֹ שֶׁמָּא תִהְיֶה לִי אַכְזָבָה?

שמעון: זֶה לְגַמְרֵי מִן הַנִּמְנָע. אֵין לִי שׁוּם סָפֵק[5] שֶׁתִּמְצָאִי כָּאן אֶת הַכֹּל עוֹד יוֹתֵר יָפֶה מֵאֲשֶׁר[6] חִפִּית לוֹ. אוּלָם הָאֳנִיָה עוֹמֶדֶת. עָלֵינוּ לָלֶכֶת מִיָּד אֶל מָקוֹם בְּקֹרֶת הַפַּסְפּוֹרְטִים. אַחֶרֶת יָכוֹל לִהְיוֹת שֶׁעָלֵינוּ לַחֲכּוֹת שָׁעוֹת. (הוֹלְכִים)…

רחל: חוֹשְׁשַׁתְנִי[7] שֶׁכְּבָר אֵחַרְנוּ. אֵיזֶה דֹּחַק! אַף פַּעַם לֹא הָיִיתִי מַאֲמִינָה שֶׁיֵּשׁ כָּל כָּךְ הַרְבֵּה אֲנָשִׁים עִמָּנוּ עַל הָאֳנִיָה.

שמעון: לַעֲזָאזֵל, יִהְיֶה עָלֵינוּ לַעֲמוֹד בַּתּוֹר. אֲנִי שׂוֹנֵא לְבַטֵּל אֶת הַזְּמָן בְּאֹפֶן כָּזֶה. אוּלָם מַה יֵּשׁ לַעֲשׂוֹת? דֶּרֶךְ אַגַּב, אַתְּ בְּטוּחָה[8] שֶׁלֹּא שָׁכַחְנוּ כְּלוּם בְּתוֹךְ הַקַּבִּינָה?

רחל: לֹא. חָזַרְתִּי בִּמְיֻחָד לִבְדּוֹק. מַה יֵעָשֶׂה[9] בַּמִּזְוָדוֹת שֶׁלָּנוּ?

שמעון: נִמְצָא אוֹתָן בְּבֵית הַמֶּכֶס. מַה קָּרָה, הַתּוֹר אֵינוֹ זָז כְּלָל? זֶה נֹעַל נֶפֶשׁ!

---

[1] §83b. [2] §111. [3] The name of a large cactus which is a prominent feature of the Palestinian landscape; slang-word for a native Palestinian.

1. IN TEL AVIV HARBOUR

Simon and Rachel are leaning over the rail and looking towards the distant shore. The boat is slowly approaching the harbour and the first lighters are making towards it.

Rachel. So this is Palestine, the land of my dreams! Who could have foretold that I should so soon have a chance of seeing it?

Simon. Anyway, you're not coming to it like a stranger. By your Hebrew nobody would guess that you are not a 'Tsabra'. You are almost a Palestinian already.

Rachel. No, darling, you're wrong. I have been a full Palestinian for a fortnight, ever since I was married to you! But it's true, I've been in this country so much in my thoughts that I feel as if I were coming home to it. And yet I can't help feeling a little afraid. Shall I find this country as I imagined it, or shall I be disappointed?

Simon. There's no question of that. I'm perfectly sure you'll find everything even better than you expected. But the boat is stopping. Quick, we must go to the passport control at once or else we may have to wait for hours. (*They go...*)

Rachel. I'm afraid we're late already. What a crush! I should never have believed there were such a lot of people on board with us.

Simon. Dammit, we'll have to stand in the queue. I hate wasting time like this. But there's nothing else for it. By the way, are you sure we haven't left anything in the cabin?

Rachel. No. I went back specially and had a look. What will happen to our luggage?

Simon. We shall find it in the customs house. What's the matter, the queue isn't moving at all. This is really too bad!

[4] § 59. [5] § 21. [6] § 55. [7] § 87. [8] § 117. [9] § 97, no. 34.

רחל: אַל תִּתְרַגֵּשׁ. אֲהוּבִי. הַבֵּט. כַּמָּה אֲנָשִׁים עוֹמְדִים מֵאַחֲרֵינוּ. אֲנַחְנוּ כִּמְעַט בֵּין הָרִאשׁוֹנִים.

שמעון: אָה. אֲנַחְנוּ מִתְקַדְּמִים לְאַט לְאַט. כַּנִּרְאֶה הַפְּקִידִים זֶה עַתָּה הִגִּיעוּ. הִנֵּה[10] כְּבָר אֶחָד פָּנוּי. בּוֹאִי. נִגַּשׁ אֵלָיו. (אֶל הַפָּקִיד:) הִנֵּה הַפַּסְפּוֹרְטִים שֶׁלִּי וְשֶׁל אִשְׁתִּי.

הפקיד: אֵיךְ זֶה שֶׁאֵין שְׁנֵיכֶם רְשׁוּמִים בְּפַּסְפּוֹרְט אֶחָד؟

שמעון: אֲנִי יְלִיד הָאָרֶץ. אֲבָל אִשְׁתִּי יְלִידַת אַנְגְלִיָּה וְשָׁמְרָה עַל נְתִינוּתָהּ גַּם אַחֲרֵי נִשּׂוּאֶיהָ[11].

הפקיד: זֶהוּ בִּקּוּרָהּ[12] הָרִאשׁוֹן בָּאָרֶץ؟ גְּבִרְתִּי؟

רחל: כֵּן. אֶלָּא שֶׁאֵין זֶה בִּבְחִינַת בִּקּוּר. בָּאתִי עַל מְנָת לְהִשְׁתַּקֵּעַ.

הפקיד: כָּךְ נָכוֹן. אֲנִי מְאַחֵל לָהּ הַצְלָחָה רַבָּה. שָׁלוֹם. אַחֵר. בְּבַקָּשָׁה.

[10] § 59.   [11] § 32.   [12] § 14.

2. בְּבֵית הַמֶּכֶס

רחל: אֵיךְ נוּכַל לִמְצֹא אֶת מִזְוְדוֹתֵינוּ בְּתוֹךְ הַתֹּהוּ־וָבֹהוּ הַזֶּה؟

שמעון: לְאַט לְאַט! נַעֲבֹר בֵּין עֲרֵמוֹת הַמִּטְעָן וּנְחַפֵּשׂ. אַתְּ תַּבִּיטִי[1] לְצַד שְׂמֹאל וַאֲנִי לְצַד יָמִין.

רחל: בֶּאֱמֶת. אֲנִי חוֹשֶׁבֶת שֶׁאֵלּוּ הֵן.

שמעון: מְצָאנוּ. עַכְשָׁו עָלֵינוּ לְהַפְנוֹת אֵלֵינוּ שִׂימַת לֵב אַחַד הַפְּקִידִים. הִנֵּה אֶחָד עוֹבֵר. (אֶל הַפָּקִיד:) בְּבַקָּשָׁה. תּוֹאִיל לִבְדֹּק אֶת חֲפָצֵינוּ. הִנֵּה כְּבָר הַכֹּל פָּתוּחַ.

הפקיד: הִנֵּה רְשִׁימָה שֶׁל הַדְּבָרִים הַטְּעוּנִים[2] מֶכֶס וְהַדְּבָרִים שֶׁאָסוּר לְהַכְנִיס אוֹתָם לָאָרֶץ. יֵשׁ אֶצְלְכֶם דָּבָר מֵאֵלֶּה؟

שמעון: לֹא. כָּל מַה שֶׁיֵּשׁ לָנוּ הֵם[3] חֲפָצִים פְּרָטִיִּים.

הפקיד: (אַחֲרֵי בְּדִיקָה בִּשְׁתֵּי מִזְוָדוֹת): בְּסֵדֶר. תִּרְאוּ אֶת הַפִּתְקָה הַזֹּאת בַּשַּׁעַר.

[1] § 78.   [2] § 130.   [3] § 99.

Rachel. Don't get excited, darling. Look how many people there are behind us. We're almost at the front.

Simon. Ah, we're getting on a bit. Apparently the officers have only just come. Look, there's one free already. Come on, let's go up to him. (*To the officer*) Please, here are my own and my wife's passports.

The Officer. How is it that you're not both travelling on one passport?

Simon. I'm Palestinian born, but my wife's British and has kept her nationality after marriage.

The Officer. Is this your first visit to Palestine, Madam?

Rachel. Yes, only it's hardly a visit. I've come to stay.

The Officer. That's the right spirit! I wish you the best of luck. Good bye. Next, please!

2. AT THE CUSTOMS HOUSE

Rachel. However shall we find our cases in all this confusion?

Simon. Wait a minute. We'll go along between the piles of luggage and look for them. You look to the left and I'll look to the right.

Rachel. Here they are, I think.

Simon. Fine. Now we'll have to try and get hold of one of the officers. There's one passing. (*To the officer*) Please will you be so good as to examine our luggage? Everything is open already.

The Officer. Here is a list of dutiable and prohibited articles. Have you got any of these on you?

Simon. No, all we have are articles of personal use.

The Officer (*after searching two cases*). All right. Show this form at the gate.

שמעון: תּוֹדָה. סַבָּל, סַבָּלוּ (סַבָּל אֶחָד⁴ נִגַּשׁ⁵) שָׂא אֶת הַדְּבָרִים הָאֵלֶּה אֶל טַכְסִי.

הסבל: כֵּן, אֲדוֹנִי. בּוֹאוּ אַחֲרַי.

רחל: לְאָן נִסַּע עַכְשָׁוּ?

שמעון: קֹדֶם כֹּל נִסַּע אֶל מִשְׂרָד ״אֶגֶד״⁶ וְנַשְׁאִיר שָׁם אֶת חֲפָצֵינוּ. אַחַר כָּךְ נֵלֵךְ לֶאֱכוֹל אֲרוּחַת הַצָּהֳרַיִם⁷ לִפְנֵי שֶׁנַּמְשִׁיךְ אֶת נְסִיעָתֵנוּ. אַתְּ בְּוַדַּאי גַם כֵּן רְעֵבָה. אֲנִי מַמָּשׁ גּוֹוֵעַ מֵרָעָב.

⁴ §35.   ⁵ §90.   ⁶ *Association*, the name of the co-operative coach-company plying between Tel Aviv and Jerusalem.

3. בְּמִשְׂרָד ״אֶגֶד״

רָחֵל וְשִׁמְעוֹן מַגִּיעִים בְּתוֹךְ טַכְסִי.

הנהג: הִגַּעְנוּ, אֲדוֹנִי. אֲכַנִּיס לְךָ אֶת הַחֲפָצִים לַמִּשְׂרָד, אִם אַתָּה רוֹצֶה.

שמעון: תּוֹדָה רַבָּה. כַּמָּה עָלַי לְשַׁלֵּם?

הנהג: שִׁבְעָה גְּרוּשׁ וָחֵצִי.¹

שמעון: הֵא לְךָ עוֹד גְּרוּשׁ אֶחָד בַּקְּשִׁישׁ.² בּוֹאִי, חֲמוּדָתִי, קְחִי אֶת אֶת קֻפְסַת הַכּוֹבָעִים, וַאֲנִי אֶשָּׂא אֶת מְכוֹנַת הַכְּתִיבָה. נִגַּשׁ לָרֶגַע כְּדֵי לְהוֹדִיעַ³ עַל אוֹדוֹת זְמַן הַנְּסִיעוֹת. (נִגָּשׁ אֶל הָאֶשְׁנָב וּפוֹנֶה⁴ אֶל הַפָּקִיד:) בְּבַקָּשָׁה, מָתַי יֵשׁ אוֹטוֹ לִירוּשָׁלַיִם?

הפקיד: יוֹצֵא⁵ מִכַּאן אֶחָד כִּמְעַט כָּל רֶבַע שָׁעָה. יֵשׁ בְּמִדּוּמֵנִי עוֹד מָקוֹם בַּזֶּה הָעוֹמֵד בַּתַּחֲנָה כָּעֵת, אֲבָל עֲלֵיכֶם לְמַהֵר.

שמעון: אֵין צֹרֶךְ⁶. אֲנִי רוֹצֶה לִנְסוֹעַ בְּעוֹד שָׁעָה בְּעֶרֶךְ. הַאִם אֶפְשָׁר לְהַשְׁאִיר כַּאן אֶת הַמִּזְוָדוֹת?

¹ The Palestinian Pound is equal to the Pound Sterling. It is divided into 1000 Mils, but the common unit of calculation is the Piastre, or Grush = 10 Mils, i.e. twopence-farthing. Half a Grush is roughly a penny. Five Grush are called a shilling.

Simon. Thank you. Porter, porter! (*A porter turns up.*) Take these things to a taxi, please.

The Porter. Very good, sir. Follow me, please.

Rachel. Where are we going now?

Simon. First of all we'll drive to the 'Egged' office and leave our luggage there. Then we'll go and have lunch before going on. I expect you're hungry, too. I'm simply famished.

[7] § 4, note 1.

3. AT THE 'EGGED' OFFICE

Rachel and Simon arrive in a taxi.

The Driver. Here we are, sir. I'll take your luggage into the office, if you wish.

Simon. Thank you very much. What have I to pay?

The Driver. Seven-and-a-half piastres.

Simon. Here you are, one piastre tip. Come on, darling, take your hat-box, and I will carry the typewriter. We'll only go in for a moment to find out about the times of departure. (*Goes up to the counter and asks the clerk*) When is there a bus to Jerusalem?

The Clerk. One leaves here almost every quarter of an hour. I believe there is still some room in the one standing in the station now. But you will have to hurry.

Simon. No, thanks, I want to travel in about an hour's time. Can I leave our cases here?

[2] A Persian word, common in the whole East. Engl. *baksheesh.* [3] See § 97, no. 31. [4] This verb means *to turn, to apply, to address, to pay attention.* [5] § 115. [6] § 108.

הפקיד: כן, כְּמוּבָן הַחֶבְרָה אֵינָהּ אַחְרָאִית לָהֶן. יָשִׂים אוֹתָן שָׁם, בַּפִּנָּה, כְּדֵי שֶׁלֹּא יַפְרִיעוּ לָעוֹבְרִים וְשָׁבִים[7].

רחל: הַאִם אֵין סַכָּנָה לַעֲזוֹב אֶת הַחֲפָצִים כָּךְ?

שמעון: אַל תִּדְאֲגִי. אִישׁ לֹא יִגְנוֹב אוֹתָן. עַכְשָׁו נֵלֵךְ לְאֵיזוֹ מִסְעָדָה בַּסְּבִיבָה. זָכוּרְנִי שֶׁיֵּשׁ אַחַת מֵעֵבֶר לָרְחוֹב שֶׁהִיא טוֹבָה לְמַדַּי.

[7] § 25.

4. במסעדה

רחל   בּוֹא, אֲהוּבִי, נֵשֵׁב אֶל הַשֻּׁלְחָן הַהוּא שֶׁעַל־יַד הַחַלּוֹן[1]. אֲנִי אוֹהֶבֶת לְהִסְתַּכֵּל בְּחַיֵּי הָרְחוֹב בִּשְׁעַת הָאֲכִילָה.

שמעון: בְּרָצוֹן. שְׁבִי כַּאן. נוּחַ לָךְ? אִם כֵּן, מַה הוּא רָשְׁמֵךְ[2] הָרִאשׁוֹן מֵאַרְצֵנוּ?

רחל: הִיא מַקְסִימָה[3]. הַשֶּׁמֶשׁ הַזֶּה, וְהַצְּבָעִים הָאֵלֶּה! כְּמוֹ חֲלוֹם. תָּמִיד חָשַׁבְתִּי שֶׁהָאֲנָשִׁים מַגְזִימִים כְּשֶׁהֵם מִתְפַּעֲלִים כָּל כָּךְ מִיֹּפִי הָאָרֶץ, אֲבָל עַכְשָׁו אֲנִי רוֹאָה שֶׁהַמְּצִיאוּת עוֹלָה בְּהַרְבֵּה עַל כָּל הַתֵּאוּרִים.

שמעון: חַכִּי עַד שֶׁתִּרְאִי אֶת יְרוּשָׁלַיִם וְתֵדְעִי מַה זֶּה יֹפִי. אוּלָם נַגֵּשׁ לָעִנְיָן. מָה אַתְּ רוֹצָה לֶאֱכוֹל?

רחל: לֹא הַרְבֵּה. אֲנִי יוֹתֵר מִדַּי נִרְגֶּשֶׁת[4] לֶאֱכוֹל אֲרוּחַת מַמָּשׁ. בְּעִקָּר אֲנִי צְמֵאָה

שמעון: וּבְכֵן נַזְמִין לָךְ מְרַק פֵּרוֹת. זֶה יָשִׁיב אֶת נַפְשֵׁךְ.

רחל: תֵּן לִי[5] לָעִיֵּן בַּתַּפְרִיט. מִיָּמַי לֹא רָאִיתִי תַּפְרִיט כָּתוּב בְּעִבְרִית. אַךְ מַה זֶּה? כִּמְעַט שֶׁאֵינִי מְבִינָה בּוֹ מִלָּה.

שמעון: אֵין זֶה פֶּלֶא[6]. אֶת[7] הָעִבְרִית הַשִּׁמּוּשִׁית לֹא כָּל כָּךְ קַל לִרְכּשׁ בְּחוּץ לָאָרֶץ. לַמְרוֹת דִּבּוּרְךָ[8] הָעִבְרִי הַשּׁוֹטֵף עוֹד תִּתְקְלִי[9] בְּהַרְבֵּה קְשָׁיִים בְּמִטְבָּח וּבַחֲנֻיּוֹת. (הַמֶּלְצַר נִגָּשׁ:) מֶלְצַר, בְּבַקָּשָׁה, חֲמִיצַת סֶלֶק אַחַת וּמְרַק פֵּרוֹת אֶחָד, וְלֶחֶם שָׁחוֹר[10].

[1] § 67.   [2] Pron. *roshméch*.   [3] Lit. *bewitching*.   [4] § 56.   [5] The verb *to give* (§ 97, no. 10) means *to allow* when it comes before another verb.

The Clerk. Yes, but of course the company is not responsible for them. Put them in that corner over there so that they won't get into people's way.

Rachel. Isn't it risky to leave the things like this?

Simon. Don't worry, nobody will steal them. Now, let's go to some restaurant near by. I remember there's a fairly good one just round the corner.

4. AT THE RESTAURANT

Rachel. Come on, darling, let's sit at that table near the window. I like looking at the life in the street while I'm eating.

Simon. Right, you sit here. Are you comfortable? Well, what's your first impression of our country?

Rachel. It's marvellous! This sun, and these colours! It's like a dream. I always thought people were exaggerating when they spoke so enthusiastically of the beauty of Palestine, but now I see that the reality is far better than any description.

Simon. You just wait until you see Jerusalem, then you'll know what beauty means! But let's come to the point. What do you want to eat?

Rachel. Not much. I'm too excited to eat a proper meal. I'm more thirsty, really.

Simon. Then I'll order you some fruit soup. That will refresh you.

Rachel. Let me have a look at the menu, please. I've never seen a menu made out in Hebrew. But what's that? I hardly understand a word of it!

Simon. No wonder. It's not so easy to get the hang of practical Hebrew outside the country. Your Hebrew conversation is fluent enough, but you will still have a lot of difficulties in the kitchen and in the shops. (*The waiter appears.*) Waiter, one beetroot soup and one fruit soup, please, and some brown bread.

[6] § 100.   [7] §§ 114, 116.   [8] § 75.   [9] § 97, no. 27.   [10] Lit. *black bread.*

המלצר: ומה אתם רוצים אחר כך‎?

רחל: תן לי צֱלִי רוסִי. זה נִרְאֶה מַאֲכָל מְעַנְיֵן.

שמעון: זה סְתָם בָּשָׂר וְתַפּוּחֵי אֲדָמָה[11], אֲבָל דֵי טָעִים. ולי בבקשה תָּבִיא גוּלָשׁ הוּנְגָּרִי ושני בַּקְבּוּקִים צוּף[12]. (המלצר מביא את המרק.)

שמעון: תודה, תן לי בבקשה מַזְלֵג אַחֵר. זה אֵינוֹ נָקִי. ואין לנו מַפִּיוֹת.

המלצר: סְלִיחָה, אדוני, אביא לכם מִיָד. (הולך.)

רחל: מרק הפרות טעים באמת.

שמעון: מוּבָן מֵאֵלָיו. זה כמעט מַאֲכָלֵנוּ הלְאוּמִי. אין צוֹרֶך[13] למחר. יש לנו פְּנָאי דֵי וְהוֹתֵר.

רחל: חֲבָל שלא נוכל לְתוּר את תל־אביב לפני שנִּצֵא.

שמעון: לא, אי־אפשר. הוֹרַי הֲרֵי מְחַכִּים לנוּ. נָשׁוּב הֵנָּה בעוד שבוע שבועַיִם[14] ונִשְׁהֶה כאן ימים אֲחָדִים. יהיה עלי לְבַלּוֹת את רוב הזמן בְּרֵאֲיוֹנוֹת עם נוֹתְנֵי עֲבוֹדָה. אבל אֲבַקֵשׁ כמה חברים שלי שֶׁיַּרְאוּ[15] לך את העיר בזמן שאני עָסוּק.

---

[11] Lit. *earth-apples*.   [12] A drink made of honey.   [13] § 107.
[14] Note: no conjunction in such phrases as *two or three*, etc.

5. פְּגִישַׁת חָבֵר

בתחנת „אֶגֶד".

שמעון: חכי כאן עד שאקנה את הכרטיסים. (הולך ושב.) עכשו נִשָּׂא את המזודות אל האוטו. נקח אותן אחת אחת. אין מה למהר, האוטו רק יצא בעוד עשרה רגעים.

רחל: הוא כמעט רֵיק. לך נא[1] וּתְפוֹס מקומות טובים בשבילנו, כדי שנוכל להסתכל בנוף בשעת הנסיעה. (איש אחד עובר, אך פתאם הוא עומד ופונה אליהם:)

האיש: חֵי נַפְשִׁי[2]! האין זה שמעון הֲרָרִי? זאת היא באמת הפתעה.

---

[1] § 77.   [2] Lit. *by the life of my soul.*

The Waiter. And what would you like to follow?

Rachel. Give me a 'Russian roast', please. That looks an interesting dish.

Simon. It's just ordinary meat and potatoes, but quite tasty. As for me, please bring me a Hungarian goulash, and two bottles of 'Tsuf'. (*The waiter brings the soup.*)

Simon. Thank you. Give me another fork, please, this one isn't clean. Also, we have no napkins.

The Waiter. I'm sorry, sir. I'll get you some at once. (*Goes.*)

Rachel. This fruit soup is really nice.

Simon. I should think it is. It's practically our national dish. You needn't hurry, we have time to spare.

Rachel. A pity we shan't be able to explore Tel Aviv before we leave.

Simon. I'm afraid that's impossible. After all, my parents are expecting us. We'll come back in a week or two and stay for a few days. I shall have to spend most of the time in interviews with employers, but I'll ask some of my friends to show you round the town while I'm busy.

[15] Like § 97, no. 51, but **her'éti, her'a**.

5. MEETING A FRIEND

At the 'Egged' Coach Station.

Simon. Wait here while I buy the tickets. (*Goes and returns.*) Now let's take the cases to the coach. We can carry them one by one. There's no need to hurry, the coach doesn't leave for ten minutes.

Rachel. It's nearly empty. Go and reserve good seats for us so that we can look at the scenery during the journey.

(*A man passes: suddenly he stops and turns to them.*)

The Man. My word, aren't you Simon Harari? That really is a surprise!

שמעון: אתה, גבריאל! כמעט שלא הִכַּרְתִּי אותך, כך השמנת. מה שלומך, חביבי?

גבריאל: כָּכָה, לא רע. חיים[3]. אבל מה אתה עושה כאן? חשבתי שאתה שוקד על לימודיך בלונדון.

שמעון: זה עתה גמרתי את לימודי. אך הבוקר הִגַּעְתִּי אַרְצָה[4]. בבקשה להכיר[5] את אשתי. זה חברי מבית הספר, גבריאל איש־שלום.

גבריאל: נעים מאד, גברתי. צריך לברך אתכם במזל טוב, אם כן. לא ידעתי שהספקת[6] להתחתן.

שמעון: התחתנו רק לפני שלושה שבועות, אחרי בחינותי.

גבריאל: זאת באמת נסיעה אִידֵיאָלִית לְיֶרַח הדְּבַשׁ. הגְּבֶרֶת[7] מבינה קְצָת עברית? האנגלית שלי לקויה מאד, לְדַאֲבוֹנִי.

רחל: כן, אני מדברת מעט.

גבריאל: זה מצוין. יהיה לך קל מאד להתאקלם[8] בארץ. אבל הרי אתם בודאי גם כן נוסעים לירושלים. נעלה. הנה האוטו הולך ונתמלא[9].

שמעון: אתה צודק. עלינו רק להטעין את מזוודותינו על המכסה.

גבריאל: ובכן אֶתְפּוֹשׂ מקומות בשבילנו, ואשוב ואעזור לכם.

[3] Lit. *one lives*; § 93.   [4] § 66.   [5] § 78   [6] § 111.   [7] Note that in Hebrew one says 'Madam' where in English one uses the proper name.

6. שיחה באוטו

גבריאל: איך הארץ מוצאת חן בעיני[1] הגברת?

רחל: עדין לא הספקתי לראות בה הרבה. סוף סוף, רק הייתי כאן שלוש שעות. אולם המעט שראיתי היה למעלה מכל תקוותי.

גבריאל: היתה לכם נסיעה נעימה?

רחל: נחמדה. הים היה שקט ואף ענן בשמים. התענגנו מאד.

שמעון: אמור לי, גבריאל. מה מעשיך? סיפרו לי[2] שקיבלת משרה טובה מאד.

[1] § 109.   [2] § 94.

Simon. Well, if it isn't Gabriel! I should hardly have recognized you, you've got so fat. How are you, old man?

Gabriel. Not too bad. But what are you doing here? I thought you were in London all this time studying hard.

Simon. I've just finished my course. I only arrived this morning. Let me introduce you to my wife. Rachel, this is my old school-friend, Gabriel Ish-Shalom.

Gabriel. How do you do? I owe you congratulations, I see. I didn't know you were married.

Simon. We were married only a fortnight ago, after my exams.

Gabriel. Well this is certainly an ideal honeymoon tour. Do you understand any Hebrew, Mrs. Harari? My English is rather poor, I'm sorry to say.

Rachel. Yes, I speak a little.

Gabriel. That's fine. It will be a great help to you in getting used to this country. But I suppose you're going to Jerusalem, too? Let's get in. The bus is beginning to fill up.

Simon. Yes, you're right. We have only to put our cases on top.

Gabriel. All right, I'll reserve seats for us and come and help you.

[8] Lit. *to acclimatize yourself.*   [9] § 84.

6. CONVERSATION IN THE COACH

Gabriel. How do you like Palestine, Mrs. Harari?

Rachel. I haven't seen much of it yet. After all, I've only been here for three hours. But the little I've seen so far has surpassed all my expectations.

Gabriel. Did you have a good journey?

Rachel. Marvellous. The sea was calm and not a cloud in the sky. We enjoyed it very much.

Simon. Tell me, Gabriel, what are you doing? I was told you got a very good job.

גבריאל : אמנם כן. אבל עזבתי אותה מזמן. עשיתי שותפות[3] עם סוחר מתכות, והעסקים לא רעים, בלי עין רעה. ביחוד מזמן פרוץ[4] המלחמה קיבלנו הזמנות די יפות מן הצבא. ומה תכניותיך אתה[5] לעתיד ?

שמעון : כאמור, גמרתי את לימודי, ועכשו אני מחפש למצא משרה כמהנדס.

גבריאל : יכול להיות שאוכל לעזור לך בזה. לכשתשוב מירושלים, סור אל משרדי, ואני אתן לך המלצות אל כמה מלקוחות[6] שלנו. מובטחני שלאחד מהם יהיה מקום למהנדס משוכלל כמוך.

שמעון : אהיה אסיר תודה לך. הביטי רחל, זהו מקוה ישראל[7], בית הספר הגדול לחקלאות.

רחל : כמה מענין. נעבור דרך הרבה מושבות יהודיות ?

שמעון : כמעט שלא. מכאן ואילך סביבה ערבית טהורה עד מוצא וקרית ענבים[8], הקרובות לירושלים. את רואה את ההרים במרחק ? אלה הם הרי יהודה.

[3] shutafut, § 24.   [4] § 74.   [5] § 19.   [6] l'kuchot.   [7] Mikvéh Israel, the oldest agricultural college, founded by the Alliance Israélite Universelle.

7. בירושלים

שמעון : חכו כאן. אלך ואביא טכסי. אתה, גבריאל, אולי גם אתה הולך בכוון רחביה ? אז תבוא אתנו בטכסי חלק מן הדרך.

גבריאל : לא, תודה. אני יורד ברחוב יפו בכוון מגרש הרוסים ?

שמעון : תשאר[1] בירושלים זמן[2] מה ?

גבריאל : לא. אין לי פנאי[2] לכך. אשוב עוד הערב, מיד כשאנמור את עסקי[3] כאן. שלום לכם. כשתהיו בתל אביב, תבואו לבקרני, לא כן ? הנה כרטים הבקור שלי.

[1] § 97, no. 27.   [2] pnai *free time*, ét *the proper time*, zman *time* in general.

Gabriel. Oh yes, but I left it some time ago. Then I went into partnership with a metal merchant, and business isn't bad, touch wood. Especially since the outbreak of war we've had good orders from the army. And what are your own plans for the future?

Simon. Well, as I told you, I've completed my course of studies, and now I hope to find a job as an engineer.

Gabriel. Maybe I can help you there. When you come back from Jerusalem drop in at my office some time and I'll give you introductions to some of our customers. I'm sure one of them will have a post open for a skilled engineer like you.

Simon. That would be very kind indeed. Look, Rachel, that's Mikveh Israel, the big agricultural school.

Rachel. How interesting. Shall we go through many Jewish colonies?

Simon. Hardly any. From here onwards we'll be passing through purely Arab country until Motza and Kiriath Anavim, just before Jerusalem. Do you see the mountains in the distance? Those are the Judaean hills.

[a] *The City of Grapes*, Kvutzah.

7. IN JERUSALEM

Simon. Wait here while I go and call a taxi. And you, Gabriel—are you perhaps going towards Rehavia, too? If so, come with us in the taxi part of the way.

Gabriel. No, thanks. I'm going down the Jaffa Road towards the Russian Square.

Simon. Shall you be staying in Jerusalem for long?

Gabriel. No, I haven't the time. I shall return to-night, as soon as I've finished my business here. Good-bye. When you come to Tel Aviv, you'll come and visit me, won't you? Here is my card.

[3] Plural, see § 42*b*.

רחל ושמעון: ברצון רב. להתראות.

שמעון: הנה טכסי אחד עובר. טכסי! (האוטו מתקרב.) בבקשה, קח את כל המזוודות האלה, והבא[4] אותנו לקרית־שאול, רחוב רבי יוחנן הסנדלר[5], מספר תשעה עשר.

הנהג: כן, אדוני. (הם נכנסים ויושבים.)

רחל: מה שם הרחוב שאנו נמצאים בו?

שמעון: זה רחוב יפו[6], הרחוב הראשי שבעיר. אמנם אין זה דוקא חלקו היותר מהודר. אבל הנה אנחנו עוברים דרך אחד הרחובות החדישים ביותר, רחוב המלך ג'ורג'[7].

רחל: הוא באמת יפה. הבנינים[8] הגבוהים האלה נותנים לא אופי אמריקאי ממש.

שמעון: הביטי, זה בנין המוסדות הלאומיים. ושכונת גנים זו מסביבנו היא רחביה.

רחל: לא תיארתי לי שישנם[9] גנים כה רעננים בארץ.

שמעון: יש ויש. אולם הם כמובן פרי עמל ממושך. את רואה, כל הקרקע בין כאן וקרית שאול היתה שממה[10] אבנים כשעזבתי את הארץ. עכשו כולה בתים וגינות.

[4] § 97, no. 50.   [5] Rabbi Yohanan the Shoemaker, famous ancient scholar.

8. בבית הורי שמעון

האם (מנשקת אותם): הכנסו נא לחדר ושבו לכם[1]. תנו לי להסתכל בכם. באמת, רחל היא בדיוק כמו שתיארתי לי אותה לפי הצילומים. יברככם השם[2] בהרבה מזל והצלחה, ילדי. אבל מה אני עומדת כאן ומפטפטת? אתם בודאי רעבים. אגיד לעוזרת שתביא[3] לכם דבר־מה לאכול.

[1] § 65.   [2] *The Name*; the name of God must not be pronounced.

78

Rachel and Simon. We'd love to. See you soon, then.

Simon. Here's a taxi passing. Taxi! (*The car comes round.*) Take all these cases and drive us to Kiriath Shaul, Rabbi Yohanan ha-Sandlar Street.

The Driver. Right, sir. (*They get into the car.*)

Rachel. What's the name of the street we're in now?

Simon. This is the Jaffa Road, the main street of the city. This isn't the most elegant part of it, though. Now we pass through one of the most modern roads, King George Street.

Rachel. It's really beautiful. The tall buildings give it quite an American appearance.

Simon. Look, this is the building of the National Institutions. And this garden suburb around us is Rehavia.

Rachel. I didn't imagine there were such flourishing gardens in this country.

Simon. There are plenty, but of course they are the result of long labour. You see, all the land between here and Kiriath Shaul was a stony waste when I left Palestine. Now it's full of houses and gardens.

[6] **Yafo.** [7] § 10. [8] **binyanim.** [9] § 103. [10] **shim'mat,** § 48.

8. AT THE PARENTS' HOUSE

Simon's Mother (*kissing them*). Come along in and sit down! Let me have a look at you. Really, Rachel is just as I imagined her from the photographs. I hope you'll be very happy and successful, my children. But what am I doing, standing here and talking? You must be hungry. I'll tell the maid to bring you something to eat.

[3] § 119.

שמעון: אל תטריחי את עצמך, אמא[4]. אכלנו ארוחה הגונה בתל אביב.

האם: אבל אתם מוכרחים לשתות כוס תה, לכל הפחות. הרי הנסיעה בכביש[5] ארוכה ומעייפת. סלחו לי רגע. (יוצאת.)

רחל: באמת נחמדה היא אמך. אני בטוחה שנתידד מהר.

האם (שבה ובידה סל גדול מלא פרות): קחו בינתים מעט פרות. בבקשה, רחל, טעמי תפוז[6]. הם באים מפרדסנו שברעננה.

שמעון: מה מצב בריאותך, אמא?

האם: ברוך השם, אין להתלונן[7]. בריאותי הוטבה[8] מאד בחדשים[9] האחרונים, מאז התרפאתי בחמי טבריה[10].—שלא אשכח לטלפן[11] לאבא. הבטחתי להודיע לו מיד כשתגיעו.

שמעון: אדבר אליו בעצמי. מה המספר?

[4] ima *Mummy*, aba *Daddy*. [5] kvish, *motor road, roadway*.
[6] Abbreviation of **tapuach zahav**, lit. *gold-apple*.

9. שיחה טלפונית

שמעון: בבקשה, שתים — אפס — תשע...

אני רוצה לדבר עם אדון הררי... עצמו. כן...

זה בנו... טוב, תודה...

כן, אבא, זה אנוכי, בנך[1] שמעון...

מצוינת. הזמן עבר כמו בחלום...

הרי תראה אותה עוד מעט, ותדון[2] בעצמך...

כן, הבאתי[3] מכתב ממנו. אספר לך על כל הנעשה בפרוטרוט[4]. חשבני שזכינו בעסק טוב. בכלל אני חושב שכדאי לפתח את קשרינו באנגליה...

לא, רחל עייפה קצת מן הנסיעה. ומכל מקום אנחנו רוצים לבלות[5] את הערב עמכם אחרי שלא התראינו זמן רב כל כך...

טוב מאד. אם כן, להתראות. אל תתעכב יותר מדי. שלום.

האם: האם אמר מתי ישוב?

[1] §48. [2] §97, no. 19. [3] §97, no. 50. [4] bi-frotrot. [5] §97, no. 41.

Simon. Don't trouble, mother. We had a good meal at Tel Aviv.

Simon's Mother. But you must, at least, have a cup of tea. After all, the journey by road is long and tiring. Excuse me, I'll be back in a minute.

Rachel. Your mother is really charming, Simon, I'm sure we shall get on well with each other.

Simon's Mother (*returning with a large basket of fruit*). Look, have some fruit while you're waiting. Do take an orange, Rachel. They're from our own orchard in Raananah.

Simon. How are you, Mother?

Simon's Mother. Thank God, I've nothing to complain of. My health has improved a lot in the last few months since I took that cure at the hot springs of Tiberias.—I mustn't forget to 'phone Father. I promised to tell him as soon as you arrived.

Simon. Let me speak to him myself. What's the number?

[7] § 106.   [8] § 97, no. 46*a*.   [9] chodashim.   [10] chamé Tvarya.
[11] l'talpén, § 97, no. 40.

9. ON THE 'PHONE

Simon. Two—o—nine, please...

I want to speak to Mr. Harari...yes, personally...

This is his son speaking...yes, thank you...

Yes, Father, it's me, your son Simon...

Splendid, the time passed like a dream...

Well, you'll see her soon, and then you can judge for yourself...

Yes, I brought you a letter from him. I'll tell you everything in detail. I think we've done very well. Altogether I believe it's worth while developing our connections in England...

No, Rachel's a little tired from the journey. And in any case we'd rather spend the evening with you after not having seen each other for such a long time...

Very good. See you soon, then. Don't stay too long. Good-bye.

Simon's Mother. Did he say when he'd be back?

שמעון: כן, אמר שיש לו ישיבה השובה בשש וחצי. אבל יצא משם בהקדם[6] האפשרי.

האם: אני יודעת את הישיבות האלו. אף פעם אינן נגמרות. אני כבר רואה שיהיה עלינו לאכול את ארוחת הערב בלעדיו[7]. אבל הנה התה. (אל העוזרת:) תודה. שימי את הכל הנה[8], על השולחן. אמזוג[9] בעצמי.

[6] hekdém.   [7] bil'adav, see § 61, last word.   [8] héna, hither.

10. שאלות הלבשה

בוקר. בחדר הזוג הצעיר. רחל יושבת לפני המראה[1] ומתפדרת. שמעון נכנס.

שמעון: עוד לא גמרת להתיפות[2]? הנה השעה עוד מעט תשע ועדיין לא אכלנו ארוחת הבוקר. האם שכחת שאנחנו רוצים ללכת העירה[3] לפני הצהרים?

רחל: אבל, אהובי, עלי רק לערוך את התסרוקת[4] שלי וללבוש שמלה, והנני מוכנה ללכת עמך לכל מקום שאתה רוצה. איזו שמלה אתה מיעץ[5] לי ללבוש? הלבנה עם הכפתורים האדומים, או בעלת הפסים[6]. אני כשלעצמי חושבת שבעלת הפסים תהיה יותר נוחה מפני ששרווליה[7] קצרים.

שמעון: את צודקת. היא גם יותר עליזה.

רחל: דרך אגב, חליפתך אינה מוצאת חן בעיני. היא נראית כל כך חמה ובלתי נוחה[8]. אתה יודע, עליך לקנות לך חליפת בד בהירה[9] כמו זו שאביך לובש.

שמעון: אבל החליפה הזאת נוחה עלי בהחלט. מלבד זה, חליפה כזאת לא תהלום אותי.

[1] mar'a.   [2] l'hityapot, § 97, no. 59.   [3] § 66.   [4] tisro'ket.
[5] Pi'el.

Simon. Yes, he told me he had an important conference at half-past six, but he'd leave as soon as he could.

Simon's Mother. I know those conferences! They never end. I can see that we'll have to have dinner without him. But here's the tea. (*To the maid*) Thank you. Put everything here on the table. I'll pour it out myself.

[9] Lit. *I shall mix.* Note that Hebrew does not express 'it.' when the object has just been mentioned.

10. DRESS PROBLEMS

In the morning, in the young couple's room. Rachel is sitting in front of the mirror and making up. Simon comes in.

Simon. Haven't you finished making yourself beautiful yet? It's nearly nine o'clock and we haven't had breakfast yet. You've not forgotten that we wanted to go to town before lunch?

Rachel. No, but darling, I've only got to do my hair and slip on a dress, then I'll be ready to go with you wherever you want. Which dress do you think I should wear? The white one with the red buttons, or the striped one? I think myself that the striped one would be more comfortable because it has short sleeves.

Simon. Yes, dear. It's gayer, too.

Rachel. By the way, I don't much like that suit of yours. It looks so hot and uncomfortable. You know, you ought to buy yourself a light linen suit, like the one your father is wearing.

Simon. But I am very comfortable in this suit and I don't feel hot at all. Besides, I shouldn't look right in that kind of suit.

[6] § 64 end.   [7] **sharvul.**   [8] § 113.   [9] **bahir** *light,* **kéhe** *dark,* of colours.

רחל: שטויות. תנסה ותראה כמה אלגנטי[10] אתה נראה. עוד היום נלך לחנות ונראה.

שמעון: טוב, אם את עומדת על כך, אני מסכים לנסות.

[10] elegan'ti.

11. בחנות

שמעון: הנה חנות הנראית[1] די הגונה. נכנס ונראה. (נכנסים, אחד המוכרים[2] נגש אליהם.)

המוכר: במה אוכל לשרת[3] את אדוני?

שמעון: רצוני לקנות חליפת בד בהירה.

המוכר: בודאי, אדוני. רק השבוע קיבלנו מבחר של חליפות יפות, איכות עידית[4] מארג תוצרת הארץ. ירשה[5] לי אדוני לקחת את מידתו. זכריה, הבא כסא בשביל הגברת! בבקשה לשבת, גברתי.

רחל: תודה רבה.

המוכר: הנה חליפה יפה. יתבונן[6]־נא, אדוני, איזו סחורה מצוינת. לא ימצא איכות שכזאת אפילו בתוצרת חוץ.

שמעון: הצבע מוצא חן בעיניך, רחל?

רחל: לפי דעתי הוא יותר מדי כהה. הייתי מעדיפה את הגון[7] של החליפה ההיא, למשל.

המוכר: אראה אם יש לנו כזה במידת אדוני. רגע אחד...אה, הנה. מתאים בדיוק. היא באמת יותר נאה. הגברת צודקת בהחלט.

שמעון: זה לא רע. הייתי רוצה ללבוש אותה.

המוכר: כמובן, אדוני. בחדר הזה, בבקשה. רגע אחד, אדליק את החשמל[8]. הכל בסדר? (שב אל רחל.) הגברת אינה מכאן, לא כן?

רחל: לא, אני נמצאת[9] כאן רק ימים אחדים.

[1] nir'ét, § 97, no. 33. [2] § 35. [3] Lit. *with what can I serve.* [4] idit.
[5] § 97, no. 51. [6] § 97, no. 57. [7] gavan.

84

Rachel. Nonsense! Try one on and you'll see how elegant you look in it. We'll go to a shop to-day and have a look.

Simon. Well, all right, if you insist, I'll try one on.

11. IN A SHOP

Simon. Here's a shop that looks quite decent. Let's go in and have a look round. (*They enter. A salesman comes up to them.*)

The Salesman. What can I do for you, sir?

Simon. I want to buy a light linen suit.

The Salesman. Certainly, sir. This very week we had in a selection of fine suits of the first quality in Palestinian material. Allow me to take your measurements. Zachariah, bring a chair for the lady. Take a seat, please, madam.

Rachel. Thank you very much.

The Salesman. Here's a nice suit. Look, sir, what excellent material. You won't find such quality even in imported goods.

Simon. How do you like the colour, Rachel?

Rachel. I think it's a bit too dark. I prefer the shade of that suit over there, for instance.

The Salesman. I'll see if we have one of that colour in your size, sir. One moment...ah, here it is. Exactly right. It really does look better, Madam is quite right.

Simon. It doesn't look bad. I'd like to try it on, though.

The Salesman. Certainly, sir. In this room here, please. One moment, I'll put on the light. Is that all right? (*He returns to Rachel*) You're not of this country, madam, are you?

Rachel. No, I've only been here a few days.

[8] Lit. *I will kindle the electricity.*   [9] § 80.

85

המוכר: איך הארץ מוצאת חן בעיניה?

רחל: לא הספקתי לראות ממנה אלא מעט, אבל אני מוצאת אותה יפה מאד. בפרט ירושלים ממש הקסימה אותי.

המוכר: כן, היא עיר יפה ביותר. דיברתי עם אנשים מארבע כנפות הארץ[10], וכל אחד התרשם מיפיה[11]. האם כבר ראתה את המושבות ואת העמק?

רחל: עוד לא. אבל אני מקוה שבקרוב תהיה לי הזדמנות לכך. הנה בעלי יוצא.

שמעון: ובכן, איך אני נראה, חביבתי?

רחל: אף פעם לא נראית כל כך אלגנטי באף חליפה. אך תסתכל בעצמך במראה ותוכח[12] כמה יפה עשית לשמוע לעצתי.

שמעון: צדקת[13]. אינני נראה כל כך משונה כמו שחשבתי. אני משער שכעבור[14] זמן־מה אתרגל לחליפה הזאת. בכמה היא עולה[15]?

המוכר: שלוש לירות וחצי, אדוני.

שמעון: זה לא ביוקר, אקח אותה.

המוכר: טוב מאד, אדוני. האם הוא זקוק לעוד דבר־מה? עניבות, חולצות, כותנות, גרבים, מטפחות, או אולי לבנים?

שמעון: לא, תודה, אין לי צורך בשום דבר כרגע. סלחי לי, רחל, אחזור ואלבש את חליפתי הישנה[16].

---

[10] Lit. *from the four corners of the earth.*   [11] yofyah, abs. yo'fi, § 42 (*d*).
[12] **tivachach**, § 97, no. 31.   [13] Lit. *you have spoken the truth.*

The Salesman. How do you like the country?

Rachel. I've seen only very little of it, but I find it most beautiful. Jerusalem especially has quite enchanted me.

The Salesman. Yes, it is a very beautiful city. I've spoken to people from all over the world and everyone is impressed by its beauty. Have you seen the colonies and the Emek?

Rachel. Not yet, but I hope I shall soon have an opportunity to do so. Here comes my husband.

Simon. Well, how do I look, darling?

Rachel. You've never looked so smart in any suit. Just look at yourself in the mirror and you'll see how wise you were to follow my advice.

Simon. You're right—I don't look as funny as I thought I would. I suppose, in time, I'll get used to this suit. How much is it?

The Salesman. Three pounds ten, sir.

Simon. That's not expensive. I'll take it.

The Salesman. Very good, sir. Do you want anything else? Ties, sports-shirts, shirts, socks, handkerchiefs, or perhaps underwear?

Simon. No, thank you, I don't need anything at the moment. Excuse me, Rachel, I'll just go and change back into my old suit.

---

[14] kaavor, § 74.   [15] § 66.   [16] yashan *old*, of a thing, zakén, of a person.

12. התיאטרון

רחל ושמעון עוברים על יד קולנוע ,,ציון" ברחוב יפו.

שמעון: אני רואה מודעה של ,,הבימה". נסתכל בה, אולי כדאי ללכת.

רחל: כן, נלך. אני כבר מתגעגעת לראות תיאטרון עברי בארץ ישראל.

שמעון: הערב[1] מציגים את ,,מות דנטון" ומחר את ,,עמך". את הראשון אינני מכיר, אבל האחרון דבר מצחיק. איזה משני המחזות את מבכרת?

רחל: אני דוקא במצב רוח לראות דבר רציני. יש לך חשק[2] ללכת הערב?

שמעון: כרצונך. אולם אני מסופק אם נצליח להשיג כרטיסים בשביל הערב. מכל מקום, ננסה[3]. (נכנסים ונגשים אל הקופה.)

שמעון: היש עוד כרטיסים בשביל הערב?

הפקידה: יש עוד אחדים בשבעה גרוש וחצי ובעשרה גרוש. אולם אלה שבשבעה גרוש וחצי כולם מקומות בודדים.

שמעון: אם כן, תני לי שנים בעשרה גרוש, אבל מקומות באמצע, אם ישנם[4].

הפקידה: הנה שני מקומות בשורה התשיעית.

שמעון: אני מצטער. יש לי רק שטר[5] של חמש לירות.

הפקידה: אין דבר, אוכל לפרוט.

שמעון: מתי תתחיל ההצגה[6]?

הפקידה: בשמונה וחצי, בדיוק.

שמעון: תודה. בואי, רחל. צריך למהר הביתה, כדי שנספיק לאכול ולהתלבש בזמן. נסע[7] באוטו. התחנה כאן, בפינה.

---

[1] § 15.   [2] chéshek, lit. *have you any desire.*   [3] § 97, no. 41.

12. THE THEATRE

Rachel and Simon pass the 'Zion' Cinema in Jaffa Road

Simon. I see a poster of 'Habimah'. Let's have a look at it. Perhaps it's something worth going to.

Rachel. Yes, let's go. I'm just longing to see a Hebrew play in Palestine.

Simon. To-night they are giving 'Danton's Death' and to-morrow 'Your People'. I don't know the first one, but the second is very funny. Which of the two plays would you prefer?

Rachel. I'm rather in the mood for seeing something serious. Would you like to go to-night?

Simon. If you like. I've my doubts, though, whether we'll be able to get tickets for to-night. Anyway, we'll try. (*They enter and go up to the box-office.*)

Simon. Are there any tickets left for to-night?

The Girl. There are still a few at seven-and-a-half piastres and some at ten piastres. But those at seven-and-a-half piastres are all single seats.

Simon. Then give me two tickets at ten piastres, please. I want seats in the centre if possible.

The Girl. Here are two seats in the ninth row.

Simon. I'm sorry I've only a five-pound note on me.

The Girl. That's all right, I can change it.

Simon. When does the performance start?

The Girl. At half-past eight sharp.

Simon. Thank you. Come on, Rachel, we must hurry home, so that we've time to eat and dress. We'll take the bus. Here's the stop, at the corner.

[4] § 103.   [5] **shtar.**   [6] § 116.   [7] § 97, no. 9.

13. רחל חולה

שמעון שב[1] מן העיר. כשהוא נכנס, הוא פוגש את אמו בפרוזדור.

שמעון: מה שלומך, אמא?

האם: טוב, תודה. אבל רחל לא היתה כשורה היום. היה לה כאב־בטן[2] והיא חלשה מאד.

שמעון: אל עליון! צריך לקרוא לרופא.

האם: כבר טלפנתי[3] לו. אני מחכה לבואו מדי רגע לרגע. רחל שוכבת במטה, אבל תוכל להכנס לראותה.

שמעון (נכנס אל חדר המטות): מה אני שומע, אהובה? מה לך?

רחל: אל תדאג[4]. אין מה לחשוש. אני משערת שזה מן החום, או אולי אכלתי דבר מה שקלקל את קיבתי. אני כבר מרגישה יותר טוב מזמן שנכנסת. שב וספר לי מה עשית היום.

שמעון: יש לי חדשות טובות. בעל בית־חרושת בחיפה כתב לאבא שדרוש לו מהנדס לשם פתיחת מחלקה חדשה, ומכיון ששמע עלי הוא רוצה שאבוא לראותו בעוד עשרה ימים, כשישוב מחוץ לארץ.

רחל: אכן[5] זה נפלא! עכשו אני מרגישה בריאה לגמרי...

שמעון: אל נא, חביבה. שכבי. צריך קודם כל לדעת מה יש לך. הנה אני שומע צלצול. זה כנראה[6] הרופא.

הרופא (נכנס): שלום לך, שמעון. אני שמח לראות אותך שוב אצלנו. אה, הנה החולה שלנו. היא נראית די שמחה, דומני שאינה סובלת ביותר.

רחל (מחייכת): בעלי זה עתה הביא לי בשורה[7] טובה. אולם המחלה באמת אינה כה נוראה.

---

[1] § 97, no. 19.   [2] k'év *pain*.   [3] § 97, no. 43.   [4] § 112.   [5] achén *indeed*.

13. RACHEL IS ILL

Simon comes home from town. As he enters he meets his mother in the hall.

Simon. How are you, mother?

Simon's Mother. I'm all right, thanks. But Rachel didn't feel well to-day. She's had pains inside and feels very limp.

Simon. Good God, we must get the doctor!

Simon's Mother. I've phoned him already and I expect him any minute now. Rachel has gone to bed, but you can go in and see her.

Simon. What's all this I hear, darling? What's the matter with you?

Rachel. Don't worry. It's nothing to be anxious about. I suppose it's the heat, or maybe I've eaten something that didn't agree with me. I'm feeling better already now you've come. Sit down and tell me what you've done to-day.

Simon. I've got good news. The owner of a factory in Haifa has written to Father that he wants an engineer to open a new department, and as he's heard about me he wants me to go and see him in ten days' time, when he gets back from abroad.

Rachel. How marvellous! Now I feel quite all right.

Simon. Don't, darling. Lie down. First we'll have to find out what's wrong with you. There, I hear the bell. That must be the doctor.

The Doctor (enters). Hello, Simon, glad to see you with us again. Ah, here's the patient! She seems quite cheerful, I can't think there's much wrong with her.

Rachel (smiles). My husband has just brought me some good news. But I don't feel really ill.

[6] k'nir'e *as it seems.*   [7] bsora *good news.*

הרופא: את מרגישה איזה כאבים?

רחל: לא. רק שלשול וחוסר תיאבון[8]. ואני חלשה, קשה לי לעמוד על רגלי.

הרופא: הראי[9] לי את לשונך. בבקשה. והדופק...טוב. תודה. האם מדדת את החום?

רחל: כן. שלושים ושבע ושש עשיריות[10]?

הרופא (קם): אין מה לחשוש. זוהי מחלה קלה שהרבה עולים חדשים נפגעים בה. תעבור במשך שלושה ארבעה ימים. תנו לה רק מאכלים קלים. כגון דיסת[11] סולת. צנימים ותה חלש. קחי את הרפואה שאני רושם לך שלוש פעמים ביום. ואל תקומי לפני שאבקר אותך שוב בעוד שלושה ימים. תודיעו לי מיד אם מצבה ישתנה לרעה.

רחל: תודה. אדוני הרופא.

הרופא: שלום. אם כן, להתראות.

[8] té'avon.　　[9] § 97, no. 51.　　[10] Centigrades.　　[11] daisat.

14. תכניות נסיעה

על שולחן חמשפחה בשעת ארוחת הצהרים

שמעון: היום העשרים לחודש. לא כן? בעשרים ושלושה עלי ללכת ולראות את ה'[1] בן־ציון בחיפה. צריך להתחיל לחשוב על נסיעתנו.

האב: אתה רוצה לקחת את רחל גם כן[2]?

שמעון: כמובן. הרי עדיין לא ראתה כלום מן הארץ. מלבד זאת הנגו כאן כבר יותר משבועיים ואחותנו אלישבע[3] שבחדרה בודאי משתוממת[4] מדוע אין אנו מבקרים אותה. הנה הזדמנות טובה לעשות זאת בדרך.

האם: מתי אתם מתכונים לצאת, אם כן?

[1] § 8.　　[2] § 122.　　[3] Elisheva.　　[4] § 97, no. 57 and § 96, note.

The Doctor. Have you any pains?

Rachel. No, only diarrhœa and lack of appetite. Also I'm weak—I find it difficult to stand up.

The Doctor. Let me see your tongue, please. And the pulse.... All right, thank you. Have you taken your temperature?

Rachel. Thirty-seven and six-tenths.

The Doctor. (*Rises.*) There's no need to worry at all. This is just a mild complaint from which many new immigrants suffer. It will pass in three or four days. Give her only light food, such as semolina pudding, rusks and weak tea. Take the medicine I prescribe for you three times a day and don't get up until I come to see you again in three days' time. Let me know at once if she should feel any worse.

Rachel. Thank you, Doctor.

The Doctor. Good bye, then, see you soon.

14. TRAVEL PLANS

At the family dinner table.

Simon. It's the twentieth to-day, isn't it? On the twenty-third I have to go and see Mr. Benzion at Haifa. We must start thinking about our journey.

Father. Do you mean to take Rachel with you?

Simon. Of course. After all, she hasn't seen anything of the country so far. Besides, we have been here more than a fortnight and it's high time she went to see her sister Elizabeth in Hadera. We shall have a good opportunity of doing that now, on our way.

Mother. When do you mean to go, then?

שמעון: מחרתים. הדרך היותר טובה היא באוטו עד לוד ומשם ברכבת[5]. נצא בעשר ועשרים לפני הצהרים. זה יתן לנו זמן מספיק לשם בקורנו לחדרה.

האב: תשובו אחרי הראיון. כמובן?

שמעון: זה תלוי בתוצאת הראיון. אולי ה' בן-ציון ירצה שאתחיל בעבודה בקרוב. אז יהיה מוטב להשאר[6] בחיפה כדי למצוא דירה ולקנות רהיטים[7] לפני שאתחיל. מכל מקום רחל או אני נשוב ליום יומים כדי לקחת את שאר חפצינו.

האב: אם תהיו עסוקים בחיפה, אין צורך להטריח את עצמכם. נוכל לשלוח לכם את הכל.

האם: חבל שעליכם לעזוב אותנו כל כך מהר. רחל ואני התידדנו כל כך.

רחל: אין דבר, אמא. אבוא הנה לבקורים קצרים מזמן לזמן אחרי שנתישב.

שמעון: כולכם מדברים כאלו[8] אני כבר מתחיל לעבוד. סוף סוף אינני הולך אלא[9] לשם ראיון. יכול מאד להיות שלא אקבל את המשרה כלל.

האב: נכון. אולם מר[10] בן-ציון נתן לי את הרושם שדרוש לו מישהו באופן תכוף. לך ישנן כל הידיעות הדרושות. ובכן, למה לא יקבל אותך?

שמעון: נראה. לא תהיה אשמתי אם לא יתן לי את המשרה.

האב: מכל מקום, תודיעו לנו מיד.
שמעון: מובן מאליו. אשלח לכם מברק[11].

[5] rakevet.   [6] § 97, no. 27.   [7] rahitim.   [8] k'ilu.

Simon. The day after to-morrow. The best way to get there is by coach to Lydda and from there by train. We'll start at 10.20 in the morning; that will leave us ample time for our visit to Hadera.

Father. You'll come back after the interview, of course?

Simon. That depends on the outcome of the interview. Maybe Mr. Benzion will want me to start work very soon and then it will be better to stay in Haifa to find a flat and buy furniture before I begin. In any case Rachel or I will be back for a day or two to collect the rest of our luggage.

Father. If you're busy in Haifa you needn't bother about that. We can send everything on to you.

Mother. It's a pity you have to leave so soon. Rachel and I were getting on so well together.

Rachel. Never mind, mother, I'll often come back for visits once we've settled down.

Simon. You're all talking as if I were already starting work! After all, I'm only going for an interview. I mayn't get the job at all.

Father. That's quite true, but Mr. Benzion gave me the impression that he needed somebody very urgently. You have all the necessary qualifications, so why shouldn't he engage you?

Simon. Well, we shall see. It won't be my fault if he doesn't give me the job.

Father. Anyway, you'll let us know at once.

Simon. Of course. I'll send you a telegram.

[9] § 60.   [10] mar.   [11] mivrak.

15. בקבוץ

בחדרה. שמעון ורחל יורדים מן האוטו שהוביל אותם מן התחנה אל מרכז המושבה. שמעון פונה אל אחד העוברים והשבים.

שמעון: סליחה, אדוני, איך מגיעים אל הקבוץ האנגלי?

האיש: זה פשוט מאד. לכו ברחוב הזה עד שתגיעו אל בית הספר. שם תפנו ימינה ואחרי מאה מטר בערך תראו לצד שמאל[1] שביל העובר בין הפרדסים. שביל זה יוביל אתכם ישר אל הקבוץ.

שמעון: תודה. זה רחוק מכאן?

האיש: לאו דוקא[2]. פחות מחצי שעה. שלום...

שמעון: הצריפים והאוהלים האלה, זה בודאי הקבוץ.

רחל: גם לי נראה כך. מה הן כל המכוניות הללו? נראה כאלו כל אנשי המקום נעקרים[3] ממקומם.

שמעון: כן, אירע[4] כאן דבר מה. מוטב שנשאל לאלישבע. לעולם[5] לא נמצא אותה בתוך כל הערבוביה[6] הזאת. סלח לי, חבר, אתה מכיר אולי את אלישבע אורנשטין?

האיש: בודאי. היא עובדת בלול. תעלו שמה, מעבר לבית האוכל וראו אם היא נמצאת שם. מכל מקום, שם יגידו[7] לכם איפה היא נמצאת.

שמעון: תודה רבה. בואי, רחל, אבל הזהרי[8] שלא תכשלי בקורות האלה המונחות כאן.

[1] smol. [2] lav davka. [3] § 97, no. 28. [4] ira.

15. AT THE KIBBUTZ

At Hadera. Simon and Rachel get off the bus that has brought them from the station to the centre of the settlement. Simon stops a passer-by.

Simon. Excuse me, sir, how do we get to the English Kibbutz?

The Man. That's quite simple. Go along this road until you come to the school. Then turn to the right, and in about a hundred metres you'll see a footpath on your left leading through the orchards. That path will bring you right up to the Kibbutz.

Simon. Thank you, is it far from here?

The Man. Not at all, barely half-an-hour's walk. Good day.

Simon. These huts and tents must be the Kibbutz.

Rachel. Looks like it to me, too. What are all those lorries doing there? It looks almost as if the whole place were moving.

Simon. Yes, something is going on here. We'd better ask for Elizabeth. We'll never find her in all this confusion. Excuse me, comrade, do you know Elizabeth Orenstein?

The Man. Certainly. She's working in the chicken run. Go up there, past the dining-hut, and see if she's there. Anyway, they'll tell you there where to find her.

Simon. Thank you very much. Come on, Rachel, but mind you don't fall over those beams lying there.

[5] § 21 end.   [6] **irbuviya.**   [7] § 97, no. 48.   [8] **hizahari.**

16. האחיות מתראות

רחל: אתה רואה את הבחורה המאכילה את התרנגולות? חושבתני שזאת היא. כן, נכון, הנה ראתה אותנו.

(אלישבע רצה לקראתם. האחיות מתנשקות.[1])

אלישבע: שלום, שמעון, נעים מאד להכיר אותך. כבר השתוממתי שאתם בוששים כל כך לבוא.

רחל: אמו של שמעון[2] לא נתנה לנו ללכת, ואני הייתי חולה כשבוע ימים. אפילו עכשו אנחנו נמצאים כאן רק על רגל אחת[3], כי הננו בדרכנו לחיפה.

אלישבע: לחיפה? מה יש לכם שם?

רחל: יש לשמעון ראיון עם בעל בית חרושת. אולי יקבל משרה.

אלישבע: אני מאחלת לכם הצלחה רבה. חבל שהנכם באים דוקא בזמן שהכל אצלנו במהפכה[4] שלמה. אינני יכולה להראות לכם איך אנחנו מסודרים כאן, מפני שבעוד ימים אחדים נצא[5] מכאן לעלות על אדמתנו בעמק בית שאן.

שמעון: אכן זה נחמד. אתם בודאי מאושרים.

אלישבע: יומם ולילה אין מדברים על נושא אחר. כמעט שאין לנו סבלנות לחכות[6].

רחל: שמעתי כל כך הרבה על ,,עליות" אלו. הייתי רוצה להיות נוכחה.

אלישבע: אני חוששת שזה בלתי אפשרי. יש סכנה ידועה, וישתתפו רק העובדים המנוסים. את הילדים נשאיר בבית אלפא עד שנהיה מסודרים יפה. אמנם יחסינו[7] עם שכנינו הערבים מצוינים כעת, אבל מי יגיד עתידות? צריך להיות מוכן לכל צרה שלא תבוא[8]. אך בואו, אראה לכם את הלול לכל הפחות.

[1] § 89.   [2] § 38.   [3] Lit. *on one foot*.   [4] mahpécha.   [5] § 97, no. 15.

16. THE SISTERS MEET

Rachel. Do you see that girl feeding the hens? I believe that's her! Yes, I was right, she's just seen us. (*Elizabeth runs towards them. The sisters kiss.*)

Elizabeth. How are you, Simon. I am very glad to meet you. I was beginning to wonder why you were so long in coming.

Rachel. Simon's mother wouldn't let us go. I was ill, too, for about a week. Even now we're only here on a flying visit, because we're on our way to Haifa.

Elizabeth. To Haifa? What takes you there?

Rachel. Simon has an interview with the owner of a factory. Perhaps he'll get a post.

Elizabeth. I wish you luck. It's a pity you've come just now, when everything is in complete confusion here. I can't show you how things are organized here, because in a few days' time we're leaving to take possession of our land in the Beisan valley.

Simon. That's grand. You must feel happy.

Elizabeth. Day and night we talk of nothing else. We've hardly patience to wait!

Rachel. I have heard so much of these 'occupations'. I'd love to be there.

Elizabeth. I'm afraid that's impossible. There's a certain amount of danger, and only the experienced workers will take part. We shall leave the children in Beth Alpha until we're fully settled. Our relations with our Arab neighbours are excellent just now, it's true, but who can tell? One must be prepared for any emergency. But come on, I'll at least show you the chicken-house.

[6] § 97, no. 41.   [7] **yachasénu**.   [8] Idiom, lit. *for every trouble that should not come.*

17. בלול

שמעון: את עובדת כאן בלול בקביעות?

אלישבע: כן. בעצם אני מנהלת את הלול. התמחיתי[1] בגידול עופות עוד בהיותי[2] באנגליה.

רחל: כמה מתוקים האפרוחים. אני רואה שיש לכם המון עופות.

אלישבע: יש לנו כשמונים תרנגולות. כשנסתדר על אדמתנו נקנה עוד. אומרים ששם האקלים יפה לעופות. אדמתנו—איזה צלצול מקסים יש למלה[3] הזאת!

רחל: זה בדיוק מה שאני מרגישה מן הרגע שעמדה רגלי על אדמת הארץ: הרגש הנפלא הזה שיכולים לאמר[4] ,,ארצנו. אדמתנו". אני ממש מקנאה[5] בך שזכית להשתתף בבנין ארצנו בעמל ידיך.

שמעון: איזה ענפים יש לכם עוד?

אלישבע: יש לנו גן ירקות וחמש פרות. אולם עד עכשו רוב החברים היו יוצאים[6] לעבודת חוץ.

רחל: איך תובילו את התרנגולות למקומכם החדש?

אלישבע: פשוט מאד. באוטו משא. אך לעת עתה עוד תשארנה כאן, עד שנבנה לול. שלוש בחורות תטפלנה[7] בהן. בעצם רצו להשאיר גם אותי כאן, אבל התחננתי לפני החברים שיתנו לי להשתתף בעליה על הקרקע. אמנם אחר כך אצטרך לשוב כדי להשגיח על הובלת[8] העופות.

רחל: את מדברת בהתלהבות כזאת. רואים שאת מוצאת סיפוק בעבודתך.

[1] § 97, no. 59.   [2] § 74.   [3] mila.   [4] § 97, no. 7.

17. IN THE CHICKEN-RUN

Simon. Are you working here in the chicken-run permanently?

Elizabeth. Yes. Really, I am supervising the chicken-run. I specialized in poultry breeding when I was still in England.

Rachel. How sweet the chicks are! I see you have a lot of birds.

Elizabeth. We have about eighty hens. Once we are settled on our own land, we shall buy some more. I'm told the climate there is good for poultry. Our own land—what an enchanting sound that word has!

Rachel. That's just what I've been experiencing ever since I landed in this country, the marvellous feeling of being able to speak of *our* country, *our* soil. I do envy you the privilege of contributing with your own labour to the upbuilding of this country.

Simon. What other activities do you go in for here?

Elizabeth. We have a vegetable garden and five cows. But most of the members have worked outside up till now.

Rachel. How are you going to transport the chickens to your new place?

Elizabeth. Oh, just on a lorry. But they will be left here for the time being, until we have built a run. Three girls will look after them. Actually they wanted to leave me here, too, but I begged the other comrades to let me take part in the occupation of the land. Still, I shall have to come back later and supervise the transport of the birds.

Rachel. You talk so enthusiastically! Obviously you find your work satisfying.

---

[5] m'kanét, § 97, no. 40.   [6] § 83*a*.   [7] t'tapélna.   [8] § 97, no. 47.

אלישבע: איזו שאלה! לו[9] ידעה אמא כמה מאושרת אהיה כאן, לא היתה
מתנגדת כל כך לעלייתי.

רחל: חושבתני שאמא בינתים השלימה אם החלטתך. ועתה, כשגם אנכי
נמצאת כאן, היא מתחילה אפילו להתענין בארץ ישראל. אולי נצליח לפתות[10]
אותה שתבוא הנה גם היא.

§ 125.   [10] § 97, no. 41.

18. חיפה. במלון

השוער: שלום אדון-גברת.
שמעון: שלום. אנחנו רוצים חדר לשנים.
השוער: בודאי. אדוני. יש לנו חדר יפה מאד בקומה השניה. עם חדר
אמבטיה פרטי ומרפסת. חמשים גרוש. עם ארוחת בוקר.

שמעון: אוכל לראות אותו?
השוער: תיכף ומיד, אדוני. הנה הבחורה תעלה עמכם. מספר עשרים
ושלושה. אני בטוח שהחדר ימצא חן בעיניכם. (עולים ונכנסים לחדר.)

שמעון: טוב. זה חדר נוח. נשכור[1] אותו.
הבחורה: הנה המפתח. האם תרצו לאכול דבר מה הערב?

שמעון: לא, אנחנו יוצאים. בבקשה להעיר[2] אותי מחר בשבע.

הבחורה: אדוני רוצה את ארוחת הבוקר בחדר או בחדר האוכל?

שמעון: אוכל[3] בחדר האוכל. אשתי בודאי תרצה לישון עד שעה יותר
מאוחרת.

הבחורה: טוב מאד, אדוני. בבקשה לרדת[4] ולהרשם בספר האורחים.
יעלו את מזודותיכם בעוד רגעים אחדים.

[1] niskor.   [2] § 97, no. 49.   [3] § 97, no. 7.   [4] § 97, no. 14.

Elizabeth. There's no doubt about that. If mother had realized how happy I was going to be here, she wouldn't have minded my emigration so much.

Rachel. I think mother has since got reconciled to your decision. Now that I'm living here, too, she is even beginning to take an interest in Palestine. Perhaps we shall be able to persuade her to come out here, herself.

18. HAIFA. AT THE HOTEL

The Porter. Good day, sir. Good day, madam.

Simon. Good day. We want a room for two.

The Porter. Certainly, sir. We have a very nice room on the first floor, with private bathroom and a balcony. Fifty piastres, with breakfast.

Simon. Can I have a look at it?

The Porter. At once, sir. Here is the maid, she will take you up. Number twenty-three. I'm sure you will like the room. (*They go upstairs and into the room.*)

Simon. All right, this is a comfortable room. We'll take it.

The Maid. This is the key. Shall you want anything to eat to-night?

Simon. No, we're going out. Please call me to-morrow at seven o'clock.

The Maid. Do you wish for breakfast in your room, or in the dining-room?

Simon. I will take it in the dining-room. My wife will probably want to sleep a little later.

The Maid. Very good, sir. Please go down and sign the visitors' book. Your luggage will be brought up in a few minutes.

19. ראיון עם נותן עבודה

שמעון: ה' בן-ציון נמצא כאן? אני רוצה לדבר עמו.
המזכירה: איזה שם אגיד לו?
שמעון: שמי הררי. הוא מחכה לי הבוקר.
המזכירה: מיד אדוני. בבקשה לחכות כאן. (שהה.) בבקשה להכנס...

בן-ציון (קם): אה, נעים מאד להכירך, אדון הררי. בבקשה לשבת. אביך ספר לי עליך. גמרת קורס להנדסה באנגליה, לא כן?

שמעון: כן, יש לי תואר אוניברסיטאי בהצטיינות, וגם דיפלומה מן "הקר- ליג"[1] שלי.
בן-ציון: עסקת גם בעבודה מעשית[2]?
שמעון: כן, על כל מתלמד לעבוד בבית חרושת במשך ימי החופש. עבדתי בשלושה בתי-חרושת שונים[3]. בכל אחד ארבעה חדשים, ואני בקי בכל עבודות מתכת.
בן-ציון: יש לך איזה נסיון בייצור מכשירים קטנים לצרכי[4] בית?

שמעון: במקרה בית החרושת האחרון שעבדתי בו היה מייצר מכשירים חשמליים לעבודות המטבח.
בן-ציון: מצוין. זה בדיוק מה שדרוש לי[5]. אני עומד לפתוח ענף חדש. למחמים[6] חשמליים, צולי טוסט, ועוד. רכשתי כמה פטנטים, אבל מה שדרוש לי עכשיו זה אדם המוכשר[7] לארגן את העבודה. אתה חושב שתוכל לעשות זאת?

שמעון: כן, אני מקוה שאוכל להביא דבר כזה לידי הצלחה.
בן-ציון: אתן לך הזדמנות להראות את יכולתך. אשלם לך שתים-עשרה לירות לחודש והעלאה[8] ברגע שהמחלקה תתחיל לעבוד כסדר. מסכים?

שמעון: ברצון. מתי רוצה אדוני שאתחיל בעבודה?

[1] § 10.   [2] maasit.   [3] § 16 end.   [4] § 42*d*.   [5] § 107.

104

19. INTERVIEW WITH AN EMPLOYER

Simon. Is Mr. Benzion in? I want to see him.

The Secretary. What name shall I tell him?

Simon. My name is Harari. He expects me this morning.

The Secretary. In a moment, sir. Please wait here. (*Returns.*) Will you come in?

Benzion (*rises*). Ah, glad to meet you, Mr. Harari. Please take a seat. Your father told me about you. You have completed a course of engineering in England, haven't you?

Simon. Yes. I have a University degree with a special distinction and a diploma from my college.

Benzion. Have you done practical work as well?

Simon. Yes, every student has to work in a factory during the vacation. I've worked in three different factories, four months in each, and am experienced in all metal-working processes.

Benzion. Have you had any experience with the production of small household appliances?

Simon. As it happens, the last factory in which I worked produced electric kitchen apparatus.

Benzion. Excellent. That's exactly what I need. I intend to open a new department for the production of small gadgets, like electric kettles, toasters, etc. I've acquired several patents, but what I need now is a man to organize the work. Do you think you'll be able to do that?

Simon. Yes, I hope I should be able to make a success of it.

Benzion. I'll give you a chance to show what you can do. I would pay you twelve pounds a month with a rise the moment the department is in proper working order. Do you accept?

Simon. Thank you, yes. When would you want me to start work?

⁶ méchamim.   ⁷ § 130.   ⁸ ha'ala'a, § 97, no. 51.

בן־ציון: נגיד בראשון, זאת אומרת בעוד שבוע. יש לכם כבר דירה?

שמעון: לא. הגענו רק אתמול. אתחיל לחפש היום.

בן־ציון: לא קל עכשו למצא דירה טובה. אולם בסביבה הזאת כמה שכונות הולכות ונבנות[9]. אני מקוה שתמצא דבר מה לא רחוק מדי ממקום עבודתך.

שמעון: תודה, מר בן־ציון. שלום.

בן־ציון: להתראות בעוד שבוע, אם כן. דרוש בשלום אביך.

[9] § 84.

20. חיפוש דירה

שמעון: הנה הכתובת שנתנו לנו: רחוב החלוץ מספר עשרים וארבע. נכנס. (מצלצלים בקומה הראשונה. בחורה פותחת את הדלת.)

שמעון: זאת היא דירת בעל הבית?

הבחורה: כן, הכנסו לחדר, בבקשה. אלך ואקרא לו...

בעל הבית: שלום. במה אוכל לשרת?

שמעון: אמרו לי שיש לאדוני דירה להשכיר.

בעל הבית: נכון. לא בבית הזה, אלא ממול[1]. הבית חדש ועוד עובדים בו, אבל הדירה הזאת כבר מוכנה לגמרי. בואו אתי ואראה[2] לכם. (יוצאים לרחוב.)

רחל: בת כמה חדרים היא?

בעל הבית: שלושה חדרים וכל הנוחיות. הזהרו. יתכן שהצבע עודנו טרי[3]. הנה הדירה. זהו החדר הגדול ביותר. הוא פונה צפונה[4], כך שהוא קריר ביום... החדר הזה מתאים לחדר מטות. אתם רואים, יש בו שני ארונות־קיר... הנה החדר השלישי.

רחל: והמטבח?

[1] mi-mul.   [2] ar'e.   [3] tari.   [4] § 66.

Benzion. Let's say on the first, that is in a week's time. Have you got a flat yet?

Simon. No, we only arrived here yesterday. I'll start looking for one to-day.

Benzion. It is not easy to find a good flat just now. However, there are several building estates growing up round here. I hope you'll find something not too far from your work.

Simon. Thank you, Mr. Benzion. Good-bye.

Benzion. See you in a week's time, then. Remember me to your father.

20. FLAT HUNTING

Simon. This is the address we were given: 24 Hechalutz Street. Let's go in. (*They ring at the ground-floor flat. A girl opens the door.*)

Simon. Is this the landlord's flat?

The Girl. Yes. Come in, please. I will go and call him.

The Landlord. Good morning. What can I do for you?

Simon. I was told you had a flat to let.

The Landlord. Quite right. Not in this house, though, but across the road. The house is new and the workmen are still in it, but this flat is already completed. If you wish, I will let you see it right away. (*They go out.*)

Rachel. How many rooms are there?

The Landlord. Three rooms and the usual offices. Be careful, the paint may still be wet. This is the flat, and this is the largest room. It faces north, so that it is cool by day. This room here is suitable for a bedroom. As you see it has two built-in cupboards. This is the third room.

Rachel. And the kitchen?

בעל הבית: הנהו. הוא קטן. אבל הרי אין צורך במקום רב בתוך מטבח.
יש בו מזוה[5] קריר וארונות קיר מרווחים[6].

שמעון: ומה שכר[7] הדירה?

בעל הבית: ארבע לירות וחצי לחודש. תצטרכו לעשות חוזה לשנתים.
אחרי זה התנאים הם ממוחרם למוחרם.

רחל: מוחרם. מה זה?

שמעון: הראשון למוחרם הוא ראש השנה המושלימית. נוהגים כאן
להשכיר דירות לפי שנה זו. ובכן, נחשוב בדבר. אם נחליט לשכור את
הדירה, נשוב בימים הבאים ונחתום על החוזה.

בעל הבית: טוב. כמובן, אינני ערב[8] שעוד תהיה פנויה. רבים הקופצים
כעת על דירה כזאת. לכן איעץ[9] לכם שלא תדחו את החלטתכם. שלום.

[5] m'zave. [6] m'ruvachim. [7] s'char *wage, payment.*

21. קניית כלי בית

שמעון ורחל יוצאים מחנות הרהיטים.

שמעון: תודה לאל שהסתפטרנו משאלת הרהיטים כל כך מהר.

רחל: האמן[1] לי. נוכל להיות שבעי רצון בקניתנו.

שמעון: הן צדקי[2]. זאת היא מציאה ממש. היה קשה לקבל רהיטים יפים
ונוחים כל כך אפילו במחיר הרבה יותר גבוה.

רחל: האם סידרת בדבר הבאת[3] הדברים לדירתנו?

שמעון: כן. יביאו אותם ביום הרביעי אחרי הצהרים. עלינו להיות שם,
כמובן, כדי להשגיח שכל דבר יעמד[4] במקומו. הערב נלך ונחליט איפה לשים
כל דבר. רשמתי אצלי את המדות.

רחל: אני שמחה לקראת עבודה זו. יש לי נטיה גדולה לסידור חדרים.

[1] § 97, no. 45, lit. *believe me.*   [2] hén tsidki, lit. *my word of faith.*

The Landlord. Here it is. It's small, but then you don't need much room in a kitchen, do you? It has a cool larder and spacious built-in cupboards.

Simon. And what is the rent?

The Landlord. Four pounds ten a month. The contract is for two years, and after that the terms are from Muharram to Muharram.

Rachel. What's that, Muharram?

Simon. The first of Muharram is the Moslem New Year's day. Flats here are usually let for that year. Well, we'll think it over. If we decide to take the flat, we'll come back in a few days' time and sign the contract.

The Landlord. All right. Of course, I can't guarantee that it will still be free. There's a great demand just now for flats like this. So if you'll take my advice you won't delay your decision too long. Good day.

⁸ arév.   ⁹ Pi'el.

21. EQUIPPING THE HOME

Simon and Rachel come out of the furniture shop.

Simon. Thank God we've dealt with the furniture problem so quickly.

Rachel. I'm sure we can be well satisfied with our purchases.

Simon. I should say so, too. It was a real bargain. We could hardly have got better or more comfortable furniture at much higher prices.

Rachel. Have you arranged about having the things sent to our flat?

Simon. Yes, they will send them on Wednesday afternoon. We'll have to be there, of course, to see that everything is put into its proper place. To-night we'll go and see where each piece is to go. I have jotted down the measurements.

Rachel. I am looking forward to that job. I just love interior decoration.

³ § 97, no. 50, verbal noun.   ⁴ § 97, no. 45 a.

שמעון: וגם כשרון, כמדומני.

רחל: מתי תחדל לעשות לי קומפלימטים[5]! אך הנה אני רואה חנות לכלי מטבח. אם רצונך בכך נכנס ונסתכל בסחורותיהם. אולי ישנם כאן דברים שכדאי לקנותם.

שמעון: רעיון טוב. יש לך הרשימה שעשינו אמש[6]?

רחל: אחפש בתיק שלי. לא, השארתי אותה על השולחן. אבל אין דבר, אם נשכח דבר, נוכל לקנותו אחר כך. את הדברים החשובים, כגון[7] סירים, מחבתים, צלחות[8], ספלים, וכדומה, אזכור גם בלי רשימה.

[5] Lit. *to make me compliments*.   [6] emesh.

22. מביאים את הרהיטים

שמעון ורחל עובדים בדירה. שמעון עומד על סולם.

שמעון: גמרתי את הוילון הזה. מה עכשו?

רחל: זה הוילון האחרון. עכשו הכל מוכן בשביל הרהיטים. אבל איפה הם? כבר שלוש וחצי, והרי אמרת לי שיביאו אותם בשלוש.

שמעון: כן, בעל החנות נשבע לי שאוכל לסמוך עליו. אלך אל החנות שבפינה ואטלפן לו. אחרבן אותו כהוגן, כשם שאני יהודי.

רחל: אל תתרגז, אהובי. חכה עוד מעט. שמע־נא, דופקים בדלת. אולי אלה הם. לך וראה. (שמעון הולך ופותח את הדלת. פועל אחד עומד בפרוזדור.)

הפועל: אנחנו באים מבית המסחר לרהיטים של זמורסקי את[1] ברנשטין. אתה האדון הררי?

שמעון: סוף סוף באתם. כבר נתיאשתי מבואכם[2].

הפועל: לא אשמתנו היא שאחרנו. מתקנים את הכביש ליד גשר מוצררה והיה עלינו לשוב ולנסוע דרך העיר.

[1] Lit. *with*.   [2] mi-bo'achem, § 74.

Simon. And you've a talent for it, too, I think.

Rachel. When will you stop flattering me! But look, there's a shop for kitchen utensils. If you like, we might go in and have a look at their goods. Perhaps there are some things worth buying.

Simon. Good idea. Have you got the list we made last night?

Rachel. I'll just look in my bag. No, I left it on the table. But never mind, if we do forget anything we can get it afterwards. As for the most important things, like pots, pans, plates, cups, and so on, I'll think of those without a list.

[7] k'gon.   [8] tsalachot, sing. tsala'chat.

22. THE FURNITURE ARRIVES

Simon and Rachel are working in the flat. Simon is standing on a step ladder.

Simon. I've done this curtain. What comes next?

Rachel. That's the last curtain. Now it's all ready for the furniture. But where is it? It's half-past three already and you told me they were bringing it at three o'clock.

Simon. Yes, and the owner of the shop promised me I could rely on him. I'll go down to the shop at the corner and 'phone him. I'll give him a piece of my mind, I can tell you!

Rachel. Don't get excited, darling. Wait just a little longer. Listen, there's somebody knocking at the door. Perhaps it's them. Go and see. (*Simon goes and opens the door. A workman is standing in the corridor.*)

The Workman. We're from Zamorski and Bernstein, the furniture dealers. Are you Mr. Harari?

Simon. So here you are at last. I'd quite given up hoping you would come.

The Workman. It isn't our fault that we are late. They're repairing the road near the Musrara bridge and we had to go back and through the town.

שמעון: נו, אין דבר. נגש לעבודה. אתה רוצה שאראה לך עכשו לאן לשים כל הדברים?

הפועל: מוטב[3] שתגיד לנו איפה להעמיד כל דבר ודבר כשאנחנו מכניסים אותו. (יורד במדרגות.)

שמעון: הנה הם מביאים את ארון הבגדים. בבקשה ממך, רחל, הדליקי את החשמל. כך. ובכן, הארון הזה נכנס לחדר שמשמאל. שימו אותו ככה, באמצע הקיר.

רחל: אתה בטוח שזהו המקום היותר טוב? הייתי שמה אותו קצת יותר רחוק מן הדלת. כאן יחסום את כל הדרך.

שמעון: נוכל להזיז אותו אחר כך. אי אפשר לדרוש מן האנשים האלה שיחכו עד שנחליט על כל פרט ופרט[4]. בין כך ובין כך לא נקבל רושם נכון עד שכל דבר נמצא[5] בחדר.

[3] mutav *it is better*.   [4] prat, § 18.

23. ב"תנובה"[1]

רחל: אני רוצה להזמין חלב בשביל הבית.

המוכר: כן, גברתי. מה השם והכתובת?

רחל: רחוב החלוץ מספר עשרים וארבע, קומה שניה.

המוכר: תודה. וכמה הגברת רוצה שנשלח כל בוקר?

רחל: ליטר[2] וחצי, בבקשה.

המוכר: טוב מאד. נתחיל מחר. זה הכל?

רחל: לא. אני רוצה לקנות חמאה וביצים.

המוכר: יש לנו חמאה בשני גרוש ובעשרים ושבעה מיל האוקיה[3].

רחל: אני רוצה חמאה מתוצרת הארץ.

המוכר: אצלנו הכל מתוצרת הארץ. אין אנו מוכרים תוצרת חוץ.

[1] The dairy co-operative.   [2] A litre is about 1¾ pints.

Simon. Well, never mind. Let's get down to work. Do you want me to show you now where everything goes?

The Workman. You'd better tell us where each piece goes as we bring it in. (*Goes downstairs.*)

Simon. Here they are, bringing the wardrobe. Put on the electric light, Rachel, please. Right. Well, this wardrobe goes into the room on the left. Put it like this, in the centre of the wall.

Rachel. Are you sure that's the best place? I should put it a bit farther away from the door. Here it'll block the whole entrance.

Simon. We can move it later. It's impossible to ask these men to wait until we have decided on every little thing. Anyway, we shan't get the right idea of what it will look like until everything is actually in the room.

[5] Lit. *is found*, frequently used for *is*.

23. AT THE 'TNUVA'

Rachel. I want to order milk for delivery at my house.

The Salesman. Yes, Madam, what name and address?

Rachel. Harari, 24 Hechalutz Street, first floor.

The Salesman. Thank you. And how much do you want sent each morning?

Rachel. One litre and a half, please.

The Salesman. Very good, Madam. We will start from tomorrow. Is there anything else?

Rachel. Yes, I want some butter and eggs.

The Salesman. We have butter at two piastres and at 27 mils the ounce.

Rachel. I want Palestinian butter.

The Salesman. All the goods we sell are Palestinian produce. We don't keep any foreign goods.

[3] The okiya is $\frac{1}{4}$ kilogram, a little over half a pound. 12 okiyot = 1 rotl.

רחל: אם כן, אקח שתי אוקיות מן החמאה שבעשרים ושבעה מיל. בכמה עולות הביצים?

המוכר: ששה גרוש וחצי התריסר[4]. יש לנו על פי רוב גם ביצים יותר זולות, אבל היום כבר אזלו.

רחל: טוב. תן לי חצי תריסר. יש לכם איזו רבה[5] טובה?

המוכר: בודאי. יש לנו רבת תפוחי זהב, רבת שזיפים, רבת דובדבנים, רבת תות השדה[6], וגם רבת ענבים. זה דבר חדש וטעים מאד. כדאי לנסות.

רחל: לא, אני מבכרת רבת תפוזים. בכמה היא עולה?

המוכר: שלושה גרוש הצנצנת[7] של שתי אוקיות ושילינג זו של ארבע אוקיות.

רחל: תן לי צנצנת של שתי אוקיות. זה הכל. כמה עלי לשלם?

המוכר: חמאה—חמישים וששה, ביצים—שלושים ושלושה, רבה—שלושים. בסך הכל שנים עשר גרוש ותשעה מילים. תני לי את אמתחתך ואשים בה את הדברים.

[4] trésar.   [5] riba.   [6] tut *mulberries*.   [7] tsintsenet.

24. בדירה החדשה

רחל: סלח־נא, שמעון יקירי, אם ארוחת הערב פרימיטיבית במקצת. מחר אני מקוה שאספיק לבשל סעודה ראויה לשמה[1].

שמעון: לפי דעתי טרחת יותר מדי בארוחה הזאת. לא היה צורך לבשל כלל, סרדינות או נקניקים, למשל, היו מספיקים בהחלט. הרי בודאי עמלת קשה במשך כל היום, מסכנה[2] שלי.

[1] Lit. *worthy of its name*.

Rachel. Then I'll have two ounces of the butter at 27 mils. How much are the eggs?

The Salesman. Six-and-a-half piastres a dozen. We usually have cheaper eggs, but to-day they are already sold out.

Rachel. All right, give me half-a-dozen, please. Have you any good jam?

The Salesman. Certainly. We have orange marmalade, plum jam, cherry jam, strawberry jam, and also grape jam. That's something new and very tasty. It's worth trying.

Rachel. No, I prefer orange marmalade. How much is it?

The Salesman. Three piastres the two-ounce jar and a shilling the four-ounce one.

Rachel. Let me have a two-ounce jar, please. That will be all. How much is that?

The Salesman. Butter, 54—eggs, 33—jam, 30: that makes 11 piastres and 7 mils. If you will give me your bag, I'll put the things in.

24. IN THE NEW HOME

Rachel. You mustn't mind, Simon darling, if the dinner is a bit primitive to-night. To-morrow I hope I shall be able to cook a proper meal.

Simon. It seems to me you've given yourself too much trouble over this meal, anyway. There was no need to cook at all, sardines or sausages would have done quite well. I'm sure you must have been very hard at work all day, you poor child.

[2] **miskén** is *poor* in the metaphorical sense only.

רחל: לא היה כל כך נורא. התימניה הבאה לעבוד היא חרוצה וזריזה ביותר ואינה זקוקה[3] כמעט להשגחה. חבל רק שלא תשאר בחיפה. עוד מעט תלך לרחובות לעזור בבית אחותה היולדת.

שמעון: בכלל אינני חושב שאשה לשעות אחדות מספיקה. הייתי מציע לשכור עוזרת ממש.

רחל: אתה בעל נחמד באמת. אודה ולא אבוש[4] שלנטרי לא הייתי מתנגדת לכך. אולם אתה בטוח שנוכל להרשות לעצמנו את ההוצאה הנוספת הזאת?

שמעון: כן. חשבתי בדבר בדרכי הביתה ובאתי לידי המסקנה שנוכל. סוף סוף יש יסוד לתקוה שאקבל האלעה בקרוב. אם כן, מחר נתחיל לחפש.

רחל: אלך אל לשכת[5] העבודה מחר אחרי הצהרים. קח עוד בשר ותפוחי אדמה, אהובי. רגע אחד, אתן לך רוטב. איך היתה עבודתך היום?

שמעון: משביעה רצון. היה נראה כאלו יהיה לנו קושי להשיג סוג ידוע של מכונות. אבל מזלי עמד לי[6]. ומצאתי מקור יותר טוב מן הראשון. אפשר שהמכונות תגענה לפני סוף החודש. אז נוכל לפתוח בעבודה.

רחל: מצאתם את הפועלים שחיפשתם?

שמעון: לא. יש לנו רק שלושה פועלים מנוסים ואת השאר נצטרך לאמן בעצמנו. אבל לזאת היה לחכות מלכתחילה. איזה מין לפתן מצוין? מה הוא?

רחל: אלה חבושים. קניתי אותם היום בתנובה. מפני שהתחנוני הילל אותם מאד. בכלל אני נהנית[7] מן הפרות הארץ־ישראליים. יש כל כך הרבה מינים חדשים בשבילי. וטעמם עולה בהרבה על זה של הפרות באנגליה.

שמעון: אקח עוד מנה, בבקשה. זה באמת דבר יוצא מן הכלל[8].

[3] § 107.   [4] évosh, lit. *I shall confess and shall not be ashamed.*

Rachel. It wasn't so bad. The Yemenite woman who comes in to work is very willing and efficient, and hardly needs any supervision. It's a pity, though, that she isn't staying in Haifa. She's going to Rechovoth soon to help in the house of her sister, who's expecting a baby.

Simon. Well, really I don't think a woman for a few hours is enough. We ought to engage a proper maid.

Rachel. You really are a charming husband! To tell you the truth, I wouldn't object at all. But are you sure we can afford the extra expense?

Simon. Yes, I thought the matter over on my way home and I've come to the conclusion that we can. After all, there's the hope that I'll get a rise soon. Well then, to-morrow we'll start looking for one.

Rachel. I'll go to the labour-exchange to-morrow afternoon. Have some more meat and potatoes, darling. Wait, I'll give you some gravy. How was work to-day?

Simon. All right. It did seem as if we should have difficulties in getting a certain type of machine. But I was lucky and found an even better supplier than the first one. Maybe the machines will arrive before the end of this month. Then we can start work.

Rachel. Did you find the workers you were looking for?

Simon. No, we've only three skilled men. The others we shall have to train ourselves. But that was to be expected all along. What an excellent sweet. What is it?

Rachel. These are quinces. I bought them to-day at the Tnuva because the shopkeeper recommended them so highly. Altogether, I do enjoy Palestinian fruit. There are so many kinds that are new to me, and it's a much better flavour than the fruit in England.

Simon. I'll have another helping, please. This is really delicious.

---

⁵ **lishkat.**   ⁶ Lit. *my lucky star stood by me.*   ⁷ § 90.   ⁸ Lit. *extraordinary.*

25. ביקור

רחל ושמעון יושבים בחדר. שמעון קורא ורחל סורגת. פתאם נשמע צלצול.

רחל: מצלצלים[1] בדלת. לך, בבקשה, אהובי, וראה מי זה.

(שמעון קם ויוצא. שומעים קולות מן המזדרון[2]. וגם רחל קמה ויוצאת.)

שמעון: הביטי, רחל. הפתעה נעימה. המהנדס קרן, חברי לעבודה, ואשתו. הכירו את אשתי.

קרן: נעים מאד להכיר את הגברת. היינו בשכונה וחשבנו שנכנס לשם שיחת חולין[3]. אני מקוה שאיננו מפריעים.

רחל: אבל לגמרי לא. שמעתי עליכם מבעלי ואני שמחה מאד להכיר אתכם. בבקשה, הכנסו ושבו.
הגב' קרן: את מדברת עברית! אכן זה נפלא. חשבתי שיהיה עלי לשבר את לשוני ולדבר אנגלית, כביכול[4].

שמעון: טעית. אצלנו בית שכולו עברי.
הגב' קרן: איזו דירה נחמדה יש לכם. הבט, יונה. איזה רהיטים יפים וחדישים. הבאתם את כל אלה מאנגליה?
רחל: לא. קנינו כל דבר כאן. כמעט הכל מתוצרת הארץ. תמהתי לראות איזה רהיטים מהודרים עושים כאן.

קרן: זה לא מפליא. הרי באים הנה בעלי־מלאכה מעולים[5] מארבע כנפות הארץ.

רחל: סלחו לי, אלך להרתיח מים לתה. עוד לא מצאנו עוזרת, ועלי לדאוג לכל דבר בעצמי.
הגב' קרן (קופצת ממקומה): אבוא לעזור לך.
רחל: לא, תודה, אין צורך. כמעט שאין מה לעשות.

הגב' קרן: כן, כן, תני לי. אפילו אם רק אדבר עמך יהיה לך יותר שמח ואני בטוחה שאמצא דבר מה לעשות.

[1] § 93.   [2] mizdron.   [3] chulin.

25. VISITORS

Rachel and Simon are sitting in their room. Simon is reading and Rachel knitting. The bell rings.

Rachel. Someone is ringing at the front-door. Please, darling, go and see who it is.

(*Simon gets up and goes out. Voices are heard from the hall, and Rachel, too, rises and goes out.*)

Simon. Look, Rachel, what a pleasant surprise. My colleague, Mr. Keren, the engineer, and his wife. Mr. and Mrs. Keren, my wife.

Keren. How do you do. We were in the neighbourhood and thought we might come in for a chat. I hope we aren't disturbing you?

Rachel. Not at all. I've heard about you from my husband and am so glad to meet you. Please come in and sit down.

Mrs. Keren. So you speak Hebrew! That's really marvellous. I thought I should have to twist my tongue in the effort to talk English, if my attempts deserve that name at all.

Simon. No, our household is strictly Hebrew.

Mrs. Keren. What a nice place you have here. Look, Jonah, what fine modern furniture. Did you bring all this from England?

Rachel. No, we bought everything here. Almost all of it is Palestinian made. I was quite surprised to see what beautiful furniture they make here.

Keren. No wonder. After all, the finest craftsmen come here from all over the world.

Rachel. Excuse me, I will go and put on some water for tea. We haven't found a maid yet, so I have to do everything myself.

Mrs. Keren (*jumps up*). Let me come and help you.

Rachel. No, thanks, it really isn't necessary. There's hardly anything to do.

Mrs. Keren. Yes, do let me. Even if I only talk to you, it will cheer you on. And I am sure I shall find something to do.

[4] ka-v-yachol, lit. *as if it could be so.*   [5] **m'ulim.**

26. שיחה מדינית

שמעון: קח סיגריה[1], קרן.

קרן: תודה. יש לכם באמת דירה יפה.

שמעון: עוד אינה מסודרת כל צרכה[2], אבל נוחה למדי. מה חדש?

קרן: היה מאמר ראשי ארוך ב,,דבר״ על המתיחות בין איטליה ואנגליה. לא אשתומם אם איטליה תכנס למלחמה עוד מעט.

שמעון: זה לא יהיה כל כך נעים בשביל ארץ ישראל.

קרן: אין דבר. תהיינה בודאי תקפות אויריות, אבל אנחנו מוכנים לכך. כבר יש לנו רשת יפה של מקלטים, ושורות ה.ג.א. מתרחבות מיום ליום. מציאות[3] צבא אנגלי גדול בקרבת הארץ מוכרחה להשפיע לטובה על התעשיה המקומית.

שמעון: ואינך מפחד מפני פלישה איטלקית?

קרן: פלישה! אולי ינסו, אבל אין לי שום ספק שלא יצליחו. אדרבה, קרוב לודאי שהאנגלים יציקו להם כהוגן, יש כאן לאנגליה אפשרות של נצחון מהיר על ארץ פשיסטית אחת. וזה יחזק את ידי כל לוחמי הדימוקרציה.

שמעון: ובכל זאת, העלה על נפשך את כל הסבל[4] אם המלחמה תגיע אל גבולות ארץ ישראל.

קרן: אינני חושב שיבוא לידי כך. וסוף סוף, אסור לנו לחשוב על עצמנו. גורלנו כיהודים תלוי בנצחון המעצמות הדימוקרטיות. אם הפשיזם יתגבר, חס וחלילה, מה יועיל לנו שהקרב[5] לא נגע בנו?

(הגב' קרן ורחל נכנסות עם מנשה[6].)

הגב' קרן: הנה שוב מתוכחים[7] על פוליטיקה. האינכם יכולים לדבר פעם גם על דברים יותר משמחים? בואו עכשו ושתו תה.

---

[1] siga'riya.   [2] kol tsorkah, lit. *as much as it needs.*   [3] m'tsi'ut, lit. *the being-found.*

26. POLITICAL CONVERSATION

Simon. Take a cigarette, Keren.

Keren. Thank you. You really have a nice place here.

Simon. It isn't quite shipshape yet, but it's fairly comfortable. What's the news?

Keren. There was a long leader in the 'Davar' on the tension between Italy and England. I shouldn't be surprised if Italy soon comes into the war.

Simon. That won't be so pleasant for this country.

Keren. Never mind. There'll certainly be some air-raids, but we're prepared for that. We've a fine system of shelters already and the number of A.R.P. volunteers is growing every day. The fact that there will be a large British army in the neighbourhood is sure to have a good effect on local industries.

Simon. And aren't you afraid of an Italian invasion?

Keren. An invasion! They'll try, maybe, but I'm sure they won't have any success. On the contrary, it's pretty certain that the English will give them a hot time. There's a chance here for England to gain a quick victory over one Fascist country, and that will be an encouragement for all who are on the democratic side.

Simon. Still, think of all the suffering if the war reaches Palestine.

Keren. I don't think it will come to that. And after all, we mustn't think of ourselves. Our fate as Jews depends on the victory of the democratic powers. If Fascism should win, which God forbid, what good will it be to us that we were not directly affected by the war? (*Mrs. Keren and Rachel come in with a tray.*)

Mrs. Keren. There they are, arguing about politics again. Can't you ever talk about more pleasant things? Now come and have some tea.

[4] sével, § 42*b*.   [5] krav.   [6] magash.   [7] mitvakchim.

27. שכירת עוזרת

רחל: ובכן את הבחורה שהגברת קרן המליצה לי עליה. מה שמך?

הבחורה: שמי חנה כהן־צדק.
רחל: בת כמה את[1], חנה?
חנה: בת תשע־עשרה, גברתי.
רחל: איזה נסיון יש לך? את יודעת לבשל?
חנה: עברתי קורס של ויצ"ו[2] בכל עבודות בית. במקומי האחרון ניהלתי את כל הבית בעצמי, מפני שהאדון והגברת יצאו שניהם לעבוד, ואני בישלתי ודאגתי לכל דבר בבית, וגם טיפלתי בילד בן תשע. הנה תעודה מן הגברת.

רחל: נראה שהיתה שבעת רצון ממך. כאן אעזור לך בעבודה, אבל אני אוהבת שהכל יהיה תמיד מבהיק ומסודר.

חנה: הגברת יכולה לסמוך עלי[3]. כמה אנשים ישנם בבית?

רחל: רק בעלי ואני. לא תמצאי את העבודה קשה ביותר. אלך לחנויות בעצמי וגם אכין[4] את רוב הארוחות. האם אמרה לך הגב' קרן שעליך לגור מחוץ לבית?

חנה: כן. אני בעצם מבכרת את זאת. אני גרה אצל הורי לא רחוק מכאן.
רחל: כמה שכר את דורשת?
חנה: במקומי האחרון קיבלתי שתי לירות וחצי לחודש.
רחל: אשלם לך כך גם כן. מתי תוכלי להתחיל?
חנה: אפילו מחר.
רחל: מצוין. אחכה לך מחר בשמונה.

חנה: בודאי. להתראות, הגברת.
רחל: עד מחר, אם כן. שלום.

[1] Lit. *a daughter of how many years are you?* Age is expressed thus with the help of bén *son* and bat.

27. ENGAGING A MAID

Rachel. So you are the girl Mrs. Keren recommended to me. What is your name?

The Girl. Hannah Kohen-Zedek.

Rachel. How old are you, Hannah?

Hannah. Nineteen, Madam.

Rachel. What experience have you had? Can you cook?

Hannah. I've done an all-round course in housework at the WIZO. In my last place I managed the whole household by myself, because the lady and the gentleman both went out to work. I cooked and ran the house, and also looked after a boy of nine. Here is a testimonial from the lady.

Rachel. She seems to have been pleased with your work. I will help you with the work here, but I do like everything to be always clean and neat.

Hannah. I'll do my best. How many people are there in the house?

Rachel. Only my husband and myself. You'll not find the work too hard. I do the shopping myself and prepare most of the meals. Did Mrs. Keren tell you that you would have to live out?

Hannah. Yes. I really prefer that. I stay with my parents not far from here.

Rachel. What wages do you want?

Hannah. In my last place I got two pounds ten a month.

Rachel. I will pay you the same. When can you start?

Hannah. To-morrow, if you like.

Rachel. Excellent. I'll expect you to-morrow morning at eight o'clock.

Hannah. Very well. Good day, Madam.

Rachel. I'll see you to-morrow, then. Good day.

---

[2] Abbreviation for *Women's International Zionist Organization.*   [3] Lit. you can rely on me.   [4] §97, no. 49.

28. שמעון רוצה להצטרף לארגון ה.ג.א.

שמעון וח' קרן יושבים במסעדה ואוכלים ארוחת הצהרים.

שמעון: שמע-נא, קרן. רציתי לשאול אותך דבר-מה. אתה חבר בה.ג.א. לא כן? אני חושב שחובה עלי להתנדב גם כן. אינני רוצה לשבת בחיבוק ידים[1] בשעת החירום.

קרן: אתה צודק בהחלט. אנשים כמוך, בעלי השכלה טכנית, מועילים במידה מיוחדת במפעלנו. מדוע אינך הולך לחרשם? מובטחני שישנו מרכז בשכונתכם. אחרי אימון של שבועות אחדים תהיה פקח.

שמעון: ומה יהיה תפקידי אז?

קרן: יהיה עליך להופיע לתרגילים מדי פעם בפעם ויותן[2] עליך תפקיד מסוים במקרה של אזעקה. אנחנו מקבלים עכשו תלבשות וכובעי פלדה בשביל החברים. הממשלה הבטיחה לשלוח לנו מדריכים מן הצבא.

שמעון: האם הקהל נענה[3] במידה מספיקה?

קרן: כן. המון מתנדבים כבר נרשמו, ורובם מסורים עד מאד. אולם דרושים לנו הרבה יותר בשביל מכבי[4] האש הנוספים ובשביל תחנות העזרה הראשונה.

שמעון: הרי בודאי ברור לקהל כמה חשוב להיות מוכנים?

קרן: בלי ספק, אבל יש לרובם צרות משלהם, כגון המשבר[5] הכלכלי, חוסר העבודה והדאגה לגורל קרוביהם באירופה. אפילו היום ישנם כאלה המאמינים שהמלחמה לא תגע[6] בנו ישר אף פעם. דרושה הרבה הסברה ותעמולה לעורר אותם לידי פעולה.

שמעון: אם כן, אלך עוד הערב לחרשם.

---

[1] Lit. *with crossed arms*.   [2] yutan, a passive form of the Kal which is only used with few verbs.

124

28. SIMON JOINS THE A.R.P. ORGANIZATION

Simon and Mr Keren are sitting at lunch in a restaurant.

Simon. Listen, Keren, I want to ask you something. You're a member of the A.R.P., aren't you? I think it's my duty to volunteer too. If an emergency does arise I don't want just to sit idle.

Keren. You're quite right. People with a technical training like yours are specially useful in our work. Why don't you go and register? I'm sure there's a centre in your district. You'll be trained for a few weeks and then you'll be made a warden.

Simon. And what will my duties be then?

Keren. You have to attend at regular intervals for practice, and you'll be given some special task in the event of a raid alarm. We're getting uniforms and steel helmets now for our personnel. The government has promised to send us some instructors from the army, too.

Simon. Are the public sufficiently interested?

Keren. Yes, a lot of volunteers have registered already, and most of them are very keen. But we need many more for the auxiliary fire brigade and the first-aid stations.

Simon. Well, surely people realize how essential it is to be prepared?

Keren. They do, but most of them have their own troubles, what with the economic crisis, unemployment, and their anxiety for their relatives in Europe. Even now there are some people who imagine the war will never affect us directly. It needs a lot of explanation and propaganda to make them more active.

Simon. I'll go and register to-night, then.

[3] § 97, no. 34.   [4] m'chabé.   [5] mashbér.   [6] § 97, no. 9.

29. חתימה

שמעון: את יודעת, אהובתי, היום עברו ששה שבועות בדיוק מזמן שהגענו לארץ.

רחל: אמנם כן, אני כבר מרגישה כאילו בילית כאן כל ימי חיי.

שמעון: גם הצלחנו די יפה. במשך ששת[1] השבועות הללו השגתי משרה, והסתדרנו בדירתנו. אך כשאנחנו מדברים על ימים נכבדים, האם שכחת שבעוד שבוע יהיו חודשים[2] מזמן חתונתנו. חושבני שצריך לחוגג יום זה.

רחל: יש לי חשק לערוך נשף ולהזמין את כל האנשים הנחמדים שהכרנו כאן.

שמעון: רעיון לא רע לגמרי. יהיה באותו זמן גם נשף חנוכת בית.

רחל: נקבע את הנשף למוצאי שבת[3]. אשב מחר לכתוב את ההזמנות.

שמעון: כמה אנשים נזמין?
רחל: את כל ידידינו. יהיה לנו די מקום. אני משערת שיהיו כעשרים איש. נכין עוגות ומשקאות[4]. חבל שאין לנו רדיו, אחרת היינו יכולים לרקוד.

שמעון: אנסה לשאול משושני את הגרמופון שלו. יש לו המון תקליטים חדשים. אלך העירה מחר להזמין יין ומשקאות אחרים.

רחל: בחיי, אני כבר שמחה לקראת כל זאת! הייתי כל כך מאושרת במשך הזמן הקצר שאני נמצאת כאן. כולם התיחסו אלי בחיבה[5] כזאת וקיבלו אותי כה יפה. לך, אהובי, כמובן מגיע עיקר התודה על הזמן הנפלא שעבר עלי.

שמעון: רגע אחד, הנני נזכר שיש לנו עוד בקבוק יין אחד בארון. הבה[6] נפתח אותו ונשתה לעתידנו בארץ הזאת.

רחל: לא, אני רוצה לשתות לעתיד ארץ זו, ארצנו. לשנה הבאה בירושלים הבנויה!

---

[1] § 68 end.   [2] § 31 b.   [3] Lit. *the outgoing of the Sabbath.*   [4] § 27 end.

126

29. EPILOGUE

Simon. You know, darling, it is just six weeks to-day since we arrived in Palestine.

Rachel. So it is. I feel already as if I'd lived here all my life.

Simon. Well, we haven't done badly. In these six weeks I've got a job and we've settled down in our home. But speaking of commemorations, have you forgotten that in a week's time we'll have been married two months? I think we ought to celebrate *that* day.

Rachel. I should like to give a party and invite all the nice people we've met here.

Simon. Not a bad idea. We'll make it a housewarming party at the same time.

Rachel. Let's have it on Saturday night. I'll sit down to-morrow and write the invitations.

Simon. How many people shall we ask?

Rachel. All our friends, we've enough room for them all. I reckon there'll be about twenty people. We'll have cakes and drinks. Pity we've no radio, otherwise we could dance.

Simon. I'll try and borrow Mr. Shoshani's gramophone. He has a lot of new records. I'll go into town to-morrow and order some wine and other drinks.

Rachel. Oh, I *am* looking forward to it all! I've been so happy the whole time I've been here. Everybody has been so nice to me, and made me so welcome. Of course you, darling, deserve most of the thanks for the marvellous time I've had.

Simon. Look here, I remember we've still got a bottle of wine in the sideboard. Let's open it and drink to our future in this country.

Rachel. No, let's drink to the future of this our country. To next year in a rebuilt Jerusalem!

[5] **chiba**, lit. *showed a relationship of liking to me.*   [6] **ha'va**, *come on.*